Women and Children in a Bengali Village

RONALD P. ROHNER

AND

MANJUSRI CHAKI-SIRCAR

Published for University of Connecticut by

UNIVERSITY PRESS OF NEW ENGLAND

HANOVER AND LONDON, 1988

UNIVERSITY PRESS OF NEW ENGLAND
Brandeis University
Brown University
Clark University
University of Connecticut
Dartmouth College
University of New Hampshire
University of Rhode Island
Tufts University
University of Vermont

Printed in the United States of America
∞

LIBRARY OF CONGRESS CATALOGING-IN-PUBLICATION DATA

Rohner, Ronald Preston, 1935–
Women and children in a Bengali village.

Bibliography: p.
Includes index.
1. Mother and child–India–Case studies.
2. Children–India–Family relationships–Case studies. 3. Maternal rejection–Case studies.
I. Chaki-Sircar, Manjusri. II. University of Connecticut. III. Title.
HQ755.85.R65 1988 306.8′743′0954 87–25463
ISBN 0–87451–431–2

5 4 3 2 1

To the memory of
Leta C. Rohner, Mother
Sandra Lee Masterson, Sister
And to
SM. Charubala Chaki, Mother
Ranjabati Sircar, Daughter

ABOUT THE AUTHORS

Ronald P. Rohner is Professor of Anthropology and Human Development at the University of Connecticut at Storrs, where he directs the Center for the Study of Parental Acceptance and Rejection. His recent books include *The Warmth Dimension: Foundations of Parental Acceptance-Rejection Theory* (1986) and *Handbook for the Study of Parental Acceptance and Rejection* (1984).

Manjusri Chaki-Sircar is a Senior Research Fellow of the Indian Council for Social Science Research. She is author of *Feminism in a Traditional Society: Women of the Manipur Valley* (1984) and contributing author to several volumes, including *India: Cultural Patterns and Processes* (1982), *Desh Binodan* (1987), and *Commemorative Volume of the Government of West Bengal, Tagore's 125th Birth Anniversary* (in press).

Contents

Illustrations

Tables

Acknowledgments

any people and organizations helped with the field research and data analyses in this book, as well as with manuscript preparation. Research on which the ethnography is based was made possible by a grant to Ronald P. Rohner (principal investigator) and to Evelyn C. Rohner (co-principal investigator) from the National Institutes of Mental Health (PHS Grant MH-33868-02). Two brief field trips to India prior to the award of this grant helped develop collaborative arrangements with Indian scholars and paved the way for the necessary approval by the Indian government to do research. Moreover these trips, made possible by grants from the National Science Foundation and the Smithsonian Institution, provided Ronald and Evelyn Rohner with experiences needed to formulate a successful grant proposal to NIMH. Subsequent to the last of these trips in 1981, Ronald P. Rohner initiated a national search for an anthropologist experienced in Indian fieldwork and fluent in both English and one of the languages of India. Manjusri Chaki-Sircar, an American-trained anthropologist and Bengali citizen, was ultimately selected to do the fieldwork, and Palashpur, West Bengal, was soon thereafter selected as the field site.

Chaki-Sircar was assisted in her fieldwork from February 1981

through October 1982 by seven research assistants: Mr. Dhananjoy Ghosh, Ms. Swapna Ghosh, Ms. Bandana Lohar, Mr. Muktipada Das, Ms. Sarbani Das, Ms. Mandira Gupta, and Mr. Ultam Ghosh. Dananjoy Ghosh and Swapna Ghosh were from high-caste families and were, accordingly, especially helpful in getting data from high-caste sections of the community. Dhananjoy was particularly effective in helping to collect economic data; Swapna was able to make careful observations on the high-caste women's world. Two "untouchable" assistants, Bandana Lohar and Muktipada Das, provided invaluable information and insights into "untouchable" sectors of the village. Two high-caste, college-educated women from outside the village–Sarbani Das and Mandira Gupta–devoted most of their time to collecting formal interviews, making systematic behavior observations, and gathering data for the socialization component of the research.

Several people at Visva Bharati University, about three kilometers from Palashpur, also made invaluable contributions to the fieldwork: Upacharya professor Amlan Dutt gave Chaki-Sircar library and other privileges at the university; her elder-brother-in-law at the university, Mr. Haima Kumar Sircar, gave her moral support and assistance whenever she needed it; Prof. Surendranath Chatterjea, cartographer in the Department of Geography, took special care in the preparation of the village map; Dr. Onkar Prasad, an anthropologist at Visva Bharati, gave Chaki-Sircar the benefit of his scholarly insights into the field setting. The manager of Visva Bharati's guest house provided her with a room from time to time, and the canteen staff there provided other appreciated amenities.

Mrs. Gita Basu, a teacher at the Palashpur school, must be especially acknowledged because she not only introduced Chaki-Sircar to the village, but she also made Chaki-Sircar's life within the area easier in innumerable little ways. Others in the village also require special mention: Mr. Ananda Ghosh, headmaster, Palashpur school, and his family; Mr. Bipad Kumar Mondal, teacher; Mr. Gurudas Bhaltacharyya, teacher, and his family; Mr. Narayan Chaltapadhayya; Mr. Shaktipada Das, *upaprahan;* Mr. Biswanalti Mukhopadhyaya; Mr. Shaktipada Chaltapadhayaya; Mrs. Laxmibala Ghosh, and Mr. Soumendra Mohon Mukhapadhaya and family. In addition to these individuals, our deepest gratitude goes to the parents of the children of this study and to the numerous others who accepted Chaki-Sircar into the community with warmth and trust.

Ranji Sircar, Chaki-Sircar's daughter, helped Chaki-Sircar throughout the research period by translating materials in the regional Bengali dialect into English, and by typing these and all other research materials. Prof. Parbati Kumar Sircar, Chaki-Sircar's husband and a geographer, spent two summers in India while the fieldwork was underway. He frequently offered critical help in the collection of data, especially regarding the economic system of the village.

Data analyses for this volume—especially analyses of socialization data—were supervised by Ronald P. Rohner. Evelyn C. Rohner did much of the statistical analyses during the early phases of this data reduction and data analysis period. William L. Cook completed most of the statistical analyses after Evelyn Rohner withdrew from the research in 1982. Significant clerical assistance in the data reduction and data analyses was given by Mary Lavigne. We thank the University of Connecticut Computer Center for providing computer time and facilities to do these analyses.

Chaki-Sircar prepared the first draft of part 1 of this book and provided valuable suggestions to strengthen other parts. R. P. Rohner edited this first draft to make it consonant in style and language with the remainder of the book which he wrote. Rohner also shepherded the final manuscript through the publication process. Preston, Rohner's son, and especially Ashley, his daughter, typed most of the manuscript on the university's word-processing system; Nancy D. Rohner, his wife, proofread multiple versions of the manuscript and helped prepare the final revisions based on the helpful criticisms of Barbara D. Miller and a second reviewer who chose to remain anonymous. The University of Connecticut Research Foundation provided assistance in typing many of the tables for the book. To all these people and agencies we owe our deepest gratitude for a job well done.

Storrs, Connecticut R. P. R
July 1987

Introduction

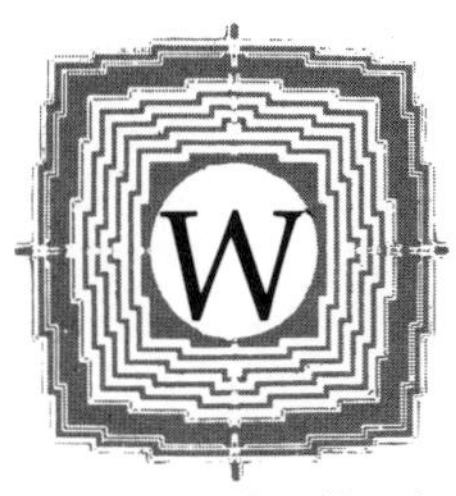

West Bengal is an understudied region of India; research on family interaction as well as major ethnographic descriptions of community life are especially lacking. Studies tend to concentrate on other specialized problems, such as Bengali rituals, marriage rules, kinship, caste, and gender roles (see, for example, Davis 1976; Fruzzetti 1982; Inden 1976; Inden and Nicholas 1977; Klass 1966; Ostor 1984; Roy 1975). This book is one of few works that study issues of family interaction within the general ethnographic context of a single Bengali community, in this case the community of Palashpur.[1]

As the title suggests, this volume focuses heavily on Palashpur women as wives and mothers, and on their six- through twelve-year-old children. Part 1 is a descriptive ethnography of the way of life in Palashpur. In addition to providing an overall ethnographic portrait of the village, this part focuses on sex-role relationships, and especially on the lives of women in both high-caste and "untouchable" families; it also focuses on intercaste dependencies, caste differences in life-style, and on intercaste tensions. This portion of the book provides the context for

1. The name Palashpur is a pseudonym for the village.

interpreting socialization data in part 2, which concentrates on the warmth dimension of parenting (i.e., on perceived maternal acceptance-rejection) and on the effects and determinants of perceived maternal acceptance in the village.

Part 2—especially chapter 7—answers such specific questions as To what extent do children (and adults) in Palashpur perceive themselves to be (or to have been, as children) accepted or rejected by their mothers? How does this general level of perceived maternal acceptance in Palashpur compare with the degree of maternal acceptance reported by children and adults in other parts of India? Do children and adults in Palashpur respond to perceived maternal acceptance-rejection as predicted by parental acceptance-rejection theory, which guided the formulation and implementation of this research (see Rohner 1975, 1980, 1986; see also chap. 6 herein)?[2] Why are some parents in Palashpur more accepting than other parents? Do children's sex and age, for example, make a difference in determining variations in a mother's warmth? Do significant caste differences exist in the experience of maternal acceptance-rejection? Inasmuch as such sex, age, and caste differences in maternal warmth do occur, what sociocultural and personal (e.g., personal stress) factors help explain them?

This book is the first full-scale ethnographic field study to test the major postulates of parental acceptance-rejection theory. It is also one of the all-too-few analyses of parent-child relations to be conducted within India. Prior work in India on parent-child relations includes seminal writings by Minturn and Hitchcock (1966), Minturn and Lambert (1964), Whiting (1963), and Whiting and Whiting (1975); all these volumes discuss the Rajputs of Khalapur in northern India. Also important here are the works of Seymour (1976, 1983) in Bhubaneswar, Orissa. Kakar (1978, 1979), Narain (1964), and Roland (1982) provide interesting if overgeneralized psychoanalytically oriented analyses of Indian parenting. Other important writings include works by Poffen-

2. The study is a part of a larger program of international research aimed at testing and refining parental acceptance-rejection theory—a theory of socialization that attempts to explain and predict major antecedents, correlates, and consequences of parental acceptance and rejection the world over. Details of the theory are provided in Rohner 1986.

berger (1981) and especially Miller (1978, 1980, 1981) on the implications of the widespread preference among Indian parents for sons versus daughters, particularly in rural northern India. This latter issue is directly relevant to the major concerns of this book, as amplified in part 2.

Ronald P. Rohner, an American anthropologist/psychologist, formulated the overall theoretical and methodological structure of the research for this book; the fieldwork component of the research was implemented by Manjusri Chaki-Sircar, an American-trained anthropologist and a citizen of West Bengal. Chaki-Sircar lived continually in the village for about twenty months, from February 1981 through October 1982, and made several visits to the village subsequent to that time. Palashpur was chosen as a field site because it fulfilled several preestablished criteria: it is a nucleated village of approximately 1,275 people, who provide most of the goods and services needed for daily living; it is small enough for its permanent residents to know of each other's existence and for them to be able to interact occasionally on a face-to-face basis; but it is large enough to provide a sample of at least fifty children in the six- through twelve-year-old age range (balanced by sex) from different families and castes. In effect, as expressed by Whiting (1966, 149) the community of Palashpur "corresponds to a 'culture' cut down to manageable size."

A team of four Bengali research assistants helped Chaki-Sircar complete the fieldwork. Two field assistants–one male and one female–were from the high-caste Satgop caste, and two were from "untouchable" castes: a woman was from the Lohar caste, and a man was from the Baen caste. In addition, Chaki-Sircar employed two local high-caste women with academic backgrounds in psychology to help with the socialization aspects of the research. Even though she herself is a citizen of West Bengal, Chaki-Sircar was often looked upon in the village as a foreigner and therefore she was not identified with any specific caste group. This was an advantage because she was treated as a visitor with whom conversations could be held without the usual caste-based inhibitions. Here intimate knowledge of the Bengali language helped her feel at ease with the people and to work with them without having to rely on bilingual informants. The nonthreatening nature of research on children and families helped her become close to adults of both sexes, which in turn eventually allowed her to observe other areas of community life as well.

Being a woman, Chaki-Sircar was somewhat limited in her access to the male world in Palashpur, but her male assistants helped greatly. Her role in the male world was further smoothed by the fictive kin relationships she assumed with some of the men—"brother," "uncle," "nephew." Reciprocally, these men addressed her by such terms as "paternal aunt" (*pishma*) or "elder sister" (*didi*). Being addressed in local kin terms eased Chaki-Sircar's way among the males as a "married daughter" of the village.

In addition to employing standard participant-observation fieldwork techniques, the field team administered to the research sample of fifty-two children and their parents a series of self-report questionnaires dealing with individuals' perceptions of maternal warmth and with their perceptions of their own personality dispositions. These instruments were validated for use in West Bengal (see the appendix). Moreover, members of the field team administered a formal parental acceptance-rejection interview schedule to both the sample children and their major caretaker—usually their mothers. The field team also conducted both formal, systematic (i.e., time-sampled), and informal behavior observations of the interaction between parents and children, as well as of the interaction between sample children and their peers. Specific details about these procedures and instruments are provided in Rohner (1984); highlights are noted here in chapter 6. Validity and reliability of the Bengali-language versions of the self-report questionnaires, on which most of the socialization analyses here are based, are presented in the appendix.

PART ONE

Living in Palashpur

CHAPTER 1

Palashpur Life Space

alashpur is a Brahman-dominated village asserting the Brahmanic ideology of male superiority. This normative ideology is internalized by women as well as men of high-caste families. For example, one Brahman priest's wife—a woman of sixty who wore a large vermillion dot on her forehead and a white sari with a bright red border[1]—announced her views about a wife's obedience to her husband: "Don't you know a woman's husband is her lord? She need not even think of any other god but him. I was married at ten. My parents did not feed me after that. He fed me." When she was jokingly reminded, "But Brahman aunt [*bamon-kakima*] he did not give this to you for free. You had to bear him seven children, and you had to cook, clean, and wash for him all your life." "And why shouldn't I?" she retorted. "I am the Laxmi [goddess of grace and prosperity worshiped at home] of his home. If I do not take care of it, the family will be deprived of joy." Other women who heard her were amused at her theatrical expression, but they did not dissent from her opinion.

1. The red-bordered sari, the vermillion-powder dot (*sindur*) on her forehead and in the middle part of her hair, conch shell bangles, and one thin iron bangle all signify the ideal image of a married woman. A widow discards these marriage symbols.

Middle-aged and elderly high-caste women in Palashpur often proclaim with pride and conviction that their role is blessed, for both motherhood itself and the role of mother are identified in Palashpur, as elsewhere in West Bengal (Roy 1975), with divinity. Wifehood too is ritualized as the role of Laxmi. Both men and women often glorify a wife's role as that of Mother Durga, the supreme goddess of strength and the destroyer of evil. Thus, even though the status of female is structurally subordinate to that of male (Davis 1976), women are not personally regarded as inferior. A young wife knows that she has to work and wait many years to achieve, at the prime of her life, the high status of a mature woman and mother. Girls face discrimination from their mothers, who favor boys, but girls seldom perceive this differential treatment as rejection or a sign of their own personal inferiority. They are socialized to be nurturant toward boys and younger siblings, giving girls a spiritually superior standing over the others. Thus, even though men in high-caste Palashpur families may enjoy normative superiority over women, women (especially older, mature women) exercise interpersonal power over men in many family decisions, as we demonstrate in later chapters.

The "untouchable" portion of the community is quite different in its social values. Outwardly, "untouchable" women conform to the customs of wearing vermillion powder and red-bordered clothing—the ideal image of a married woman—but in reality they do not conform to the implications of these symbols in the Brahmanic ideology. Normatively, "untouchable" men hold a superior status over "untouchable" women, but in daily life women frequently defy male-oriented rules, and unlike high-caste women they often leave their husbands and take their children with them. "Untouchable" men and women enjoy an egalitarian relationship, where women bear the economic burden equally with men. An untouchable wife's role is not mystified with the same spiritual aura as that of a Brahman wife, but reverence for motherhood is nonetheless perpetuated in the untouchables' religious world. Whereas high-caste marriages are indissoluble, marital separation is a common phenomenon in untouchable marriages. An untouchable woman cannot depend on her husband for her living. From childhood onward she develops self-reliance that, if her marriage works, helps her share the economic burden of the family alongside her husband; if her marriage fails, she has to find her own way financially, and she often has to take care of her children too.

Because of their sociostructural superiority over women, both high-caste and untouchable men enjoy certain social advantages. Men are vested with legitimate authority in land transactions and inheritance, and women laborers are paid less than men for equal work. However, despite their social advantages, Palashpur men are not generally domineering toward women. As we indicated earlier, both caste groups imbue motherhood with a religious aura of mother worship. Untouchable festivals such as Bhadu express the tender affection of a father toward his unmarried daughter; Manasha-worship songs express devotional praise for a mother, and in *bolan* songs untouchable men identify themselves with Gopis—the milkmaids of Vrindavana—in a mood of feminine devotional love. This concept of feminine devotion also pervades high-caste Vaisnavite thought. Brahmanic ideology of the religiosity of motherhood is expressed during the cycle of festivities in the village, described later. Such spiritual significance of femininity helps men create affective bonds with women as mothers, daughters, sisters, and wives.

It would be wrong to suggest that this idealized model provides a total picture of the sociocultural system of Palashpur. On the contrary, some women in high-caste homes are miserable and sometimes rebel, often hopelessly. And among the untouchables, the egalitarian relationship of the sexes is sometimes overridden by male attempts at dominance, which is positively sanctioned by the values of the high castes. In this way harmonious intersex relationships in Palashpur are often disrupted.

In a complex social atmosphere such as the one found in Palashpur, it is important to note that the socialization process differs not only between the sexes but between the two major caste strata, that is, between high-caste and untouchable families, as detailed in part 2. Also, different castes within each strata differ to some degree in their sex-role ideologies, according to their social position in the hierarchy. These matters are amplified later.

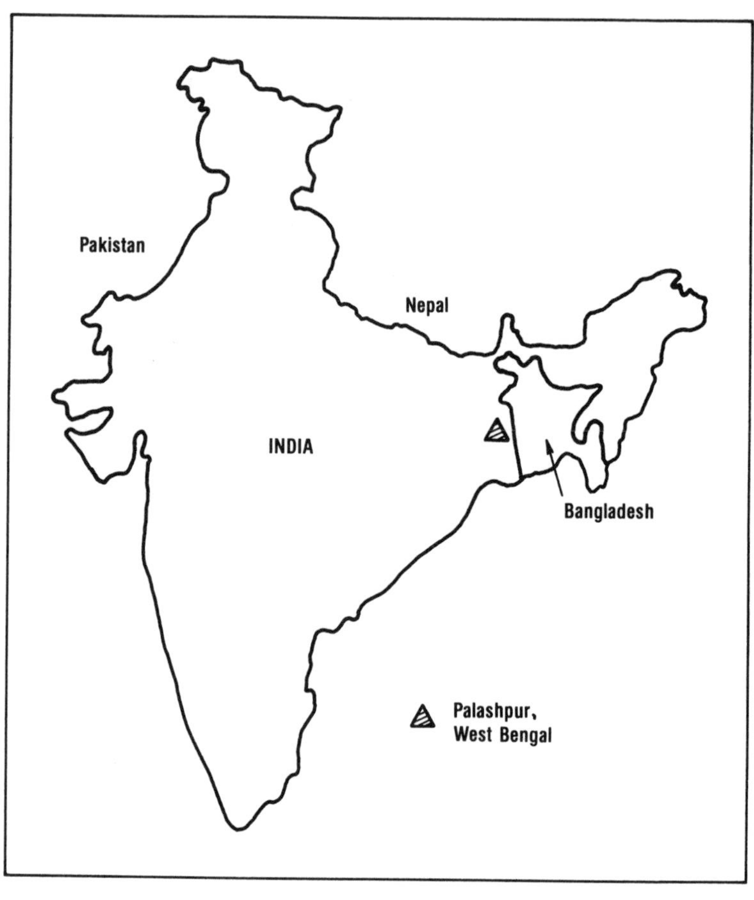

FIGURE 1. Palashpur within India

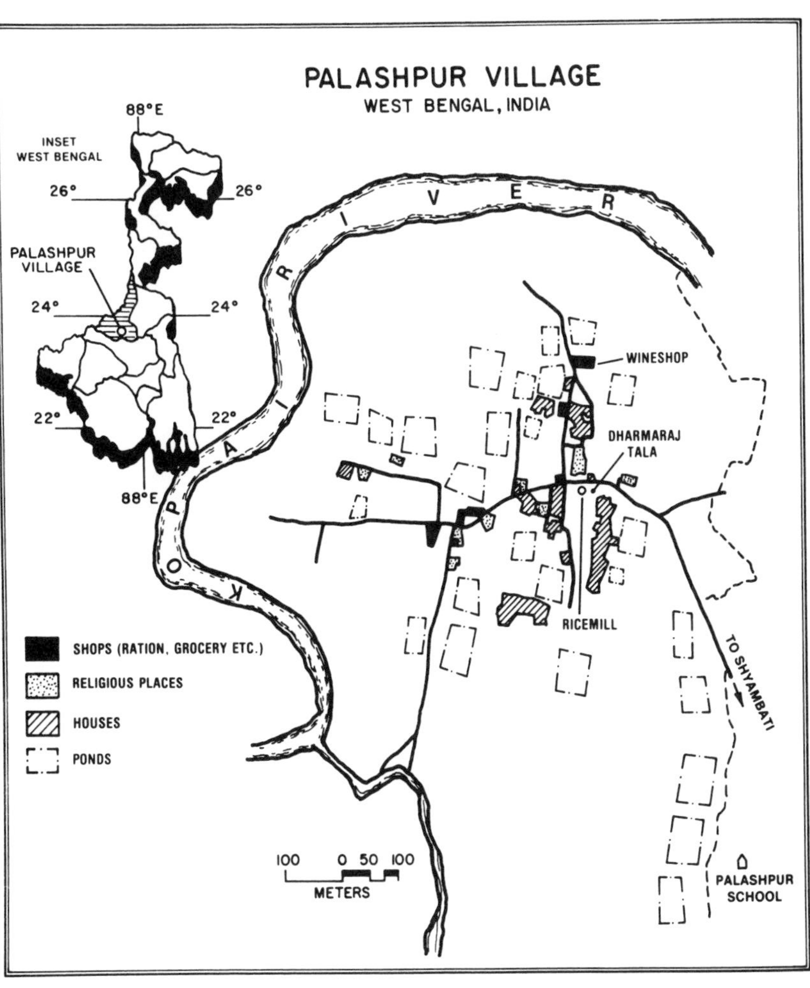

FIGURE 2. Palashpur village

The Village of Palashpur

Figure 1 shows Palashpur's approximate location within India, and figure 2 shows the village's location within West Bengal. The village covers about 359 acres; paddy fields and pastures surround the central area.[2] The village, with a population of about 1,275 people, is divided into two major sections, namely Pubpara (eastern ward) and Paschimpara (western ward). In the official block development map, Pubpara is called Palashpur, and Paschimpara is called Kabimohanpur, but both together are identified as Palashpur by local residents. The village houses 138 households belonging to fifteen different castes.[3] Pubpara has 89 households and Paschimpara has 49 households. There are six shops and six temples in Pubpara, and three shops and five temples in Paschimpara. Forty-six ponds of varying sizes dot the landscape around the village. Many were dug during the time of housebuilding. Sometimes a cluster of houses belongs to a particular caste, and the area is named by referring to that caste. For example, the untouchable Lohar live in Loharpara, fourteen untouchable Baen or Muchi families live in Muchipara, and five high-caste Satgop families live in Satgoppara. Some neighborhoods contain a mixture of castes. In Paschimpara, for example, Brahman homes often share boundary walls with untouchable Baen families of Muchipara, and Brahman households are scattered throughout the middle of the congested Lohar neigh-

2. Eighty-four of these 359 acres are irrigated from a canal; 87 acres are unirrigated; and 81 acres are unarable. Forest covers 103 acres, and cultivable wasteland covers 4 acres (Government of India, 1971 census).

3. A decade earlier the official (1971) census showed 985 people living in 181 households. The caste breakdown was as follows:

	Male	*Female*	*Total*
High caste	–	–	514
Untouchables	136	115	251
Tribals	100	120	220

No tribal person lived in the village from 1981 to 1983 when the fieldwork for this book was conducted, nor does any resident of Palashpur recall the presence of any tribal persons within the community. We suspect that some untouchables were mistakenly taken as tribal members.

borhood. Even though people of different castes live in close proximity based on social relationships of mutual dependence, they are hierarchically very much apart from each other.

High-caste and untouchable homes differ from each other in specific ways. Although most houses in Palashpur are built of mud, straw, and sometimes brick, with thatched or tin roofs, most untouchable families live in single-storied mud and thatched huts consisting of one room approximately ten-feet square where all family members sleep. Occasionally, a larger room is divided into two by a bamboo-mat partition. The huts have narrow, shaded porches, a corner of which is used for a kitchen. The porch is used for dining, storage, and as a sitting area. Sometimes three or four untouchable families build huts around a courtyard, which is used commonly for cooking and other family activities. If the family can afford it, a cow shed may be placed at one corner of the courtyard. High-caste homes, on the other hand, are usually larger, and most are two storied with three to five rooms. The front porch is used as a parlor, and the kitchen is built as a separate hut, with a porch for dining. Unlike the homes of untouchable families, high-caste houses have their own private courtyards surrounded by boundary walls.

Palashpur is surrounded by paddy fields, with patches of palmyra palm and date palm trees scattered around. Huge shady tamarind, banyan, and jam trees and mango groves grow outside the village. The soil is ideal for *palash* trees, which blossom with bright orange flowers during February and March. A *palash* forest stands on the western edge of the village (a historic spot where Tagore—in 1913, Bengal's Nobel laureate—came to celebrate Holi, the festival of colors).[4] Few trees stand within the village itself, and the houses have little room for vegetable or flower gardens, though tiny kitchen gardens are planted in some courtyards.

4. The festival of colors was introduced by Tagore at Visva Bharati in a more refined and spiritual form than the way it is performed elsewhere in India. The Visva Bharati festival is marked by music, a dance procession with students and staff in bright orange and yellow clothes, and recitation dedicated to the spirit of spring. Tagore seemed to want to involve the villages in a traditional festival, refined by discipline and an aesthetic sense.

FIGURE 3. The village of Palashpur

The main staple food is paddy (rice), grown only once a year. Cows, buffalos, goats, and some sheep are the main livestock found in most high-caste households. These animals are cared for by poorer untouchable villagers. The Dom and Handi (untouchable) castes raise chickens and pigs. Ponds belonging to high-caste families are a regular source of fish. Women and girls from the untouchable portion of the community are allowed to catch only small fish. Edible greens, mushrooms, snails, and conches are available throughout the year, but they are especially abundant after the rainy period. These food sources provide a substantial supplement to the diet of poorer segments of the community.

Palashpur's climate is of the monsoon type. In the summer months—from the end of March through April and May—the temperature can go up to 104° F, with scorching sun and dry, hot wind. Occasionally, the temperature shoots up to 109° F, and violent thunderstorms break out in the late afternoon. The monsoon starts around the beginning of June and lasts until the end of August, with sharp easterly winds and heavy torrential rain, followed by milder weather with few showers during the next three months – September through November. December, January, and February are the winter months, with the temperature going down to 50° F, and even 40° F on occasion.

Palashpur in Its Environs

Palashpur is near Santiniketan, a place known internationally for its university, Visva Bharati, founded in 1905 by the most revered poet of India, Rabindranath Tagore. Tagore attracted not only educated middle-class Indian scholars, philosophers, musicians, artists, and dancers, but his vision of modern India inspired great leaders such as Mahatma Gandhi and Pandit Nehru, all of whom addressed him as their *gurudeva* (teacher). Guided by Tagore's humanist philosophy of education, renowned personages from both the West and Far East gathered in Santiniketan to help develop the university. Tagore developed a creative environment in which middle-class, high-caste women could participate in both academic and aesthetic pursuits, which had been very much frowned upon previously. After several hundred years of subjugation (and seclusion from the public sector) by Brahmanic ideology and later by Islamic orthodoxy, high-caste women began to pursue activities alongside men at Visva Bharati. Through this process, Santiniketan became a seat of learning and vision for modern India.[5]

Tagore tried to incorporate the surrounding communities, including the tribal Santals, into his scheme, and he gradually formed a village development project by encouraging rural crafts, cottage industries (especially weaving), medical facilities, and education. Palashpur, being an adjacent community about three kilometers from Santiniketan, had great potential to benefit from Visva Bharati. Today's older people in Palashpur had witnessed many visits from Tagore and other famous men such as Gandhi, Sarojini, and Naidu. Several efforts were made to include Palashpur in the development projects. A health clinic was opened, for example, and with the help of Visva Bharati, a

5. Indira Gandhi, for example, was sent by her father to study in Santiniketan for two years.

women's craft center and a women's association were created. One teacher from Sriniketan (a village cottage-industry center some distance from Visva Bharati) opened a weaving class for local people. About twenty years ago, however, all these efforts failed. At present there remains only a night school for children and an adult education class sponsored by Visva Bharati but run poorly by local teachers. Attendance at these programs is almost negligible. Parents often complain that their children do not learn to read even after four years of school. Ironically, Palashpur now has at least minimal contact with Santiniketan through students and occasional foreign scholars who visit the Lohar-run liquor shop or toddy huts on the outskirts of the village.

Despite its closeness to Santiniketan, Palashpur has remained resistant toward Visva Bharati's rural development program. In fact, Santiniketan is often branded by Palashpur residents as the "Christian place" because they believe it has a demoralizing influence on Hindu society by allowing young men and women to work together or women to engage in public dance and musical performances.[6] The headmaster of the local school, an outsider to the village, said of the village:

> It is like the darkness under a lamp. Some other villages in this area, like Adityapur, took advantage of Santiniketan. They sent their children to schools and colleges at the university. Many now hold good jobs there. But Palashpur Brahmans were too suspicious of Tagore's activities. So they rejected any help that came from Visva Bharati. After all these years we have only five people working there; only two have decent clerical jobs. Others work in maintenance only. The attitude is changing since national independence, but people appear to have missed the good opportunities. Other villages are way ahead of Palashpur.

The village thus provides an example of a traditional community undergoing reluctant change in the face of the challenge of modernization.

6. One of the authors, Chaki-Sircar, had to keep her identity as an Indian dancer (her second profession) a secret lest the people of Palashpur become prejudiced against her.

Beyond Santiniketan, Bolpur is the nearest township, about four kilometers away. At present eight boys and one girl walk or bicycle to attend Santiniketan school, and a few go to Bolpur for high school and college, as well as for shopping, movies, or employment. During the past ten years, six moviemakers (two during the course of fieldwork for this ethnography) chose Palashpur as a location for filming, stirring a sensation in the community. (The film *Distant Thunder,* by Satyajit Ray, is widely known.) In some of the movies local people were asked to participate in minor roles or to perform as extras without payment, though some were offered bottles of foreign liquor. High-caste women declined the offer, but some untouchable Baen women were filmed during their rice planting. One of the women said, "We were not paid, but once I received a sari and a color photograph of Palashpur." Residents do not see this as exploitation, but rather enjoy the excitement and take pride in the village becoming a popular site for moviemakers. Despite these intrusions from the outside, Palashpur shows few signs of modernization. There is no high school, health clinic, drug store, or public transportation. Only two houses have septic tanks. (People are accustomed to using the fields for their toilet needs.) Few have electricity. There is one junior high school, one prebasic school, and one junior basic school. One hundred twenty-four students averaging fourteen years of age attend the junior high there. Of these, 63 are boys and 61 are girls. Junior basic has 150 students who are about eight to nine years of age. Of these, 80 are boys and 70 are girls. Prebasic school students have an average age of five to six years; the school consists of 40 students, with 25 boys and 15 girls. The three schools are located in one small brick and two thatched-roof huts. Students from surrounding villages also attend Palashpur schools. Cycle-rickshaws from Santiniketan, bullock carts, and bicycle are the main modes of transportation into Palashpur. People walk to the nearest rail station at Prantik, a tiny station with only a small platform, about two-and-one-half kilometers southeast of the village.

About two kilometers south of the village, toward Santiniketan, there is a large water canal with a forest plantation by it. The

CHAPTER 2

Making a Living in Palashpur

Land Distribution and Occupation

alashpur is an agricultural village, with high-caste landowners comprising one large group of people and untouchable landless laborers comprising another. The average high-caste landowner in Palashpur owns about three to four *bighas* of land, which must support three to ten family members—though at least four families in the village own over fifty *bighas* each. (A *bigha* is equivalent to approximately four-tenths of an acre.) Three or four *bighas* of land produce only half the year's food needs for many high-caste families. Landowners are often nostalgic about former times when they had ample land, but this must have been a long time ago because, according to Roy (Ali, 1960:47), even in the early 1930s "there [was] not enough land to go round. . . . Hardly anybody [got] enough either for his upkeep or for his fulltime engagement."

The main reasons given for deteriorating economic conditions of high-caste (usually Brahman) families relate to the need to divide land among sons after the father's death, and the need of a family to sell land in order to meet the heavy pressure of the dowry system. In addition, high-caste families generally appear apathetic to the need to improve their methods of cultivation and to invest in land—even when cash becomes available when a son marries and receives a lump sum in dowry. Moreover, landowners often complain about not getting enough yield from their land, but villagers from a nearby district often remark about the landowners of Palashpur, "They have ample land to do double cropping each year, but few of them care." Land on the Palashpur side of the Kopai River is scantily cultivated in the winter, whereas at Shihalal—a nearby village on the other side of the river—one can see vast fields in the wintertime, with sun-ripened mustard seed, sugarcane, and potatoes.

Very few high-caste people show interest in raising their income by working hard. One landowner's widow said, "We tried to grow sugarcane and grain, but the produce was stolen. Young people came and ate them up." Another high-caste man said, "I can have ample potatoes on my four *bighas* of land. But who is going to guard the field? It is too expensive to appoint a guard." This man had two unemployed grown-up sons, but he felt he could not ask them to guard the fields because such activities are usually done by untouchable men. Each year the landowners collectively appoint a guard for the rice fields. Young Baen men build small huts and stay throughout the night with bows and arrows to protect the fields. During the period of rice cultivation all landowners pool their funds to appoint a group of untouchable men as guards. No such effort is made for double cropping in the wintertime, hence it becomes difficult for a single individual to afford the services of a guard.

Landowners' lack of interest in agricultural advancement became apparent during the agricultural season of 1982, when, for the first time in memory, the rains failed to come. A few showers helped the untouchable laborers plow and sow the seed, but then came a long period of drought. Poor laborers waited in vain to start their work in the fields. This was a time when landowners could have installed shallow pumps at a cost of five to six thousand rupees each, but no one took the initiative. When asked why two or three families could not join together to buy a pump, the answer was, "There will be too much disagreement over the timing." People waited and waited for the rains to come, and with sheer disbelief they watched the lush green paddy fields turn yellow. The rivers, the ponds, and the canal all dried up. At this time the six shallow pumps that had already been installed in the village also became ineffective. In the beginning of August the villagers heard that if the rains came they could save only 50 percent of their crop; toward the end of August they heard that about 25 percent of the yield could be saved; at the end of September people stopped hoping. They realized nothing could be done. For some, famine was imminent.

The drought hit the untouchable landless cultivators the hardest. As expressed by one untouchable woman, "It is not just the money we earn from work in the fields, but we also get fish, snails, and greens—almost an entire meal—from the fields. We lost that too." Poor cultivators borrow money every year from the landowners before the agricultural season. This money is generally paid back during the agricultural season with the wages earned. This year, however, the poor earned no money to pay back. Instead they had to borrow again. But the small landowners were also seriously affected. Many of them could not offer the expected paddy to their contract laborers. Even though it is considered unethical for Brahmans to deny loans to their own *bhagchasi* or *kirshan* (i.e., contract laborers), this year most of the small landowners were unable to offer loans.

Occupational Structure Associated with Caste Stratification

Traditionally the land was owned almost totally by high-caste Brahmans and by several lower-echelon high-caste households. The rest of the population served them as hired or contract laborers. Caste stratification of the village (see table 1) is most visible in the occupational groupings that control the economic system of the community. Occupations of the castes are described in table 1.

High Castes

BRAHMANS. All Brahmans in Palashpur are landowners who depend on land for paddy, though they may not receive a year-round supply from their own fields. Those with less land lease

TABLE 1 Caste Structure in Palashpur

CASTE STRUCTURE (FROM HIGHEST TO LOWEST)	NUMBER OF HOUSEHOLDS
High castes	
(1) Brahman	48
(2) Kayastha	1
(3) Satgop	5
(4) Banik or Bene	3
(5) Tambuli	6
(6) Napit	1
(7) Sakaro	1
(8) Sundi	2
(9) Kaivarta	2
(10) Chhutor	7
(11) Kamar	2
"Untouchable" castes	
(12) Lohar	32
(13) Dom	4
(14) Handi	10
(15) Baen or Muchi	14

the land of others. In addition, some Brahman men officiate as priests for high-caste families and community rituals catering to clientele from areas farther away. Some work as professional cooks for village festivals, weddings, and funeral feasts. A handful of Brahman men hold salaried jobs in Visva Bharati University, local schools, and government offices. A few have opened snack shops catering to customers of a liquor shop in the village. One large rice-mill is owned by a rich Brahman household. Traditionally, Brahman women did not work outside the home, but today four Brahman women hold salaried positions. One is a nurse, two are village school teachers, and one is an office clerk.

KAYASTHA. The sole Kayastha male in the village holds a salaried job as a school orderly. Kayastha women do not normally work outside the home.

SATGOP. The Satgop are dependent on land, as are the Brahmans, but two Satgop men also hold salaried jobs. Satgop women generally do not work outside the home, but two unmarried Satgop girls hold temporary jobs.

BANIK or BENE. Banik men were traditionally traders. Today these men in Palashpur own a grocery shop, a rice mill, and tea stalls. They also own land. Banik women usually do not work outside the home, but one girl of twelve helps her older brother at a tea stall.

TAMBULI. Traditionally known as betel-leaf cultivators, the Tambuli today are a landowning caste. One man has a salaried job, and others own a grocery shop and tea stalls. Tambuli women usually do not work outside the home, but recently one woman started working part time as a village social worker.

NAPIT. Napit men as well as women were traditionally known as barbers. Now this occupation is followed only during ceremonial events. Napit men own and till their own land; women do not work the land but they work for other high castes during family rituals. For example, they manicure both mother and baby six days after childbirth.

SAKARO. Today the Sakaro partially depend on land. One male member of the family, however, follows the hereditary occupation of goldsmithing in a Bolpur shop. Two others are engaged in tailoring outside the village. Sakaro women do not, as a rule, work outside the home.

SUNDI. Men in one Sundi family own a large, flourishing liquor shop and a distillery. They cater to men from the untouchable castes as well as to Santal tribesmen from the surrounding area. This is the hereditary occupation of the Sundi caste. High-caste men from Palashpur also buy drinks from the shop even though they may not sit with the poor, untouchable customers. Men in this Sundi family also own a considerable amount of land. The other Sundi family has little land, and the man in the family has a salaried job. Women generally do not work outside the home.

KAIVARTA. One man engages in the hereditary occupation of fishing. Because of his unreliable income (he is an alcoholic), his wife, mother, and daughter work as domestics in Santiniketan. In the other family, the man is a schoolteacher and owns some land. Women of this family do not work outside the home.

CHHUTOR. All Chhutor families follow their hereditary occupation of carpentry. Besides making parts for bullock carts and plows, men of these families are skilled at making images of Hindu deities. In this capacity the men serve people of the village as well as the surrounding area. Next to the liquor business, the carpentry shop is the most flourishing enterprise in the village. It is indispensable for rural life in Palashpur. Women of these families work on their own land alongside the men, but one Chuttor woman has become a nurse, one is a schoolteacher, and the third holds a cleaning job at Visva Bharati University.

KAMAR. Both Kamar families engage in their hereditary craft of iron smithing. Women, too, help men make tools, and both men and women work in their own fields.

Untouchable Castes

LOHAR. Both sexes among the Lohar work as hired manual laborers in agriculture and domestic service for high-caste homes. They also raise chickens and pigs, besides taking care of livestock, for example, cattle, goats, and sheep, belonging to high-caste families.

DOM. The Dom provide the same services as the Lohar, as well as doing some fishing and basket making.

HANDI. The Handi too work as landless laborers and domestics for high-caste families. In addition, Handi men officiate as priests for the ritual sacrifice of pigs for local ceremonies. Women are traditionally midwives, an occupation rarely seen at present, though villagers still depend on these women to care for the new mother and infant during their few days of ritual seclusion immediately following the birth.

BAEN or MUCHI. The Baen were traditionally known as drummers and the Muchi were cobblers, but today not all Baen drum and no Muchi works as a cobbler. Because they work with cowhide, and because they were known to have eaten beef in the remote past, the Muchi and Baen castes are separated from the other untouchable castes. Together they are viewed as the lowest rung in the overall caste structure. At present the Baen and Muchi are all landless cultivators.

Stability and Change in the Economic Structure

As seen above, few men and women of the high castes, especially among the Brahmans, work in cultivation. However, men from the Napit, and both men and women of the Chhutor and the Kamar castes—three castes from lower-echelon high castes—work on their own land. Recently one Brahman family started tilling its own soil for the first time in the history of Palashpur. Also at present high-caste women are beginning to take salaried jobs. This too is a new phenomenon arising out of economic need, because earning from the land is not sufficient for many families. Currently, salaried jobs are considered the most prized occupations, in addition to the possession of land. Unemployed high-caste women are eager to have white-collar jobs, not out of a spirit of emancipation but because of economic pressure. High-caste men too seek jobs for themselves and also encourage their women to seek salaried jobs, albeit their attitude regarding the Brahmanic ideology of women's subordination remains unchanged. A decade ago a family of six with fifteen to twenty *bighas* of land was considered well-off. But today, according to one Brahman landowner (who is also a clerk at Visva Bharati), "even if you own a hundred *bighas* you may be like a fakir, because of the *bargadar* system."[1] "You have to have a salaried job

1. The *bargardari* system is described later, but in this context it is important to

with at least five hundred rupees salary," he continued, "just to survive." According to this man, a family of six may be said to be "all right" or "getting along" if they own fifteen *bighas* of land and if one member earns a salary of five hundred rupees. Of the forty-eight Brahman families in Palashpur, only twenty meet this criteria. A family of six with fifteen *bighas* but no salaried position is said "not to have much food." The average high-caste family of six in Palashpur subsists without a salaried position and with only six or seven *bighas* of land.

Only three Brahman families and one Banik family are considered to be rich in Palashpur. Each owns approximately seventy *bighas* of land, and each is able to maintain an on-hand cash reserve of five thousand to six thousand rupees. Two other families in this village – one Sundi and one Tambuli – are thought to be moderately rich. Both own about thirty *bighas,* and both own businesses within the village.

Until about twenty years ago when a few Brahmans received formal education and sought jobs outside the village, Palashpur Brahmans had never worked to earn a salary. At present fourteen Brahmans and twelve other high-caste men hold salaried jobs. But because of the high rate of unemployment and the lack of proper skills and education, Palashpur is full of idle high-caste men who contribute nothing to agricultural labor or to any other manual labor. In nearby districts, on the other hand, high-caste men – especially the Satgop – often work or supervise workers in the fields during the agricultural season. This is seldom done in Palashpur. In fact high-caste men of Palashpur joke, "Tell your wife to serve breakfast soon so that you can go to the fields to supervise the work. But meet us here for a card game."

The traditional occupational structure is gradually breaking down in Palashpur. As a result, Brahmans are beginning to open tea shops or grocery stores, which were originally run only by the Banik traders. Five high-caste women have taken salaried jobs; a small grocery store is now run by an old Sundi woman;

---

point out that under this system a high-caste landowner cannot readily sell his land or even borrow money against it.

and one Banik and one Brahman girl help in family tea shops. As has always been true, most high-caste women in Palashpur perform their own domestic chores, but a few engage part-time domestics to do some cleaning and washing. High-caste women cook two hot meals a day, fetch water from the tap, clean dishes, and wash clothes at the community pond. Many also boil paddy and dry it in huge quantities after the harvest. They save money by not hiring untouchable women to perform this job. Every woman in Palashpur, rich or poor, must learn how to prepare puffed rice, which is made twice a week. This is used in large quantities for breakfast and snacks. Women are also solely responsible for family laundry; men contribute nothing to household chores in high-caste homes.

The economic life of untouchables is very different from high-caste families. Untouchable men have four kinds of contractual economic relationships with the high-caste landowners.

Mahinder System

An untouchable boy starts at an early age (around nine years) as a domestic servant in a high-caste landowner's household. He receives three meals a day, a fixed salary of two rupees monthly (worth about twenty-six cents), and clothing twice a year. There are different ways of payment to a *mahinder.* An adult *mahinder* receives two meals and about twenty kilograms of paddy a month for his dinner, as well as seven to ten rupees monthly, plus two vests and two *loongis* (i.e., saronglike clothing) a year. Often a *mahinder* takes his afternoon meal, which is always served with a large quantity of rice, to his home and shares it with other members of his family. A *mahinder* works all year round, cultivating land when he is old enough to use a plow. He also plasters and paints his *manib*'s house, repairs the thatched roof, and takes care of his *manib*'s livestock.[2] Many *mahinders* enjoy a permanent relationship with their *manibs* throughout their lives. From this relationship they receive special benefits

2. *Manib* means "a master," hence the employer and the employee have an asymmetrical, hierarchical relationship.

such as gifts and money during family ceremonies. A *mahinder* goes back to his own family in the evening but he returns very early the next morning to feed his *manib*'s cattle.

The number of adult *mahinders* found in high-caste homes today is decreasing because adult untouchable men often find it hard to maintain their families with such jobs. The job of *mahinder* for a boy, though, is considered secure since this ensures clothing and food for the rest of his life if he wishes. Traditionally a *mahinder* was thought of as a part of the high-caste family. The *manib*'s children addressed him as elder brother (*dada*) or uncle (*kaka*). The *manib* was also obligated to look after the *mahinder* at the time of a crisis in the latter's family and to lend the *mahinder* money if needed. Such reliance on the *manib* is gradually diminishing, however, because *manib* landowners have less land than in former times and many can hardly afford to maintain a *mahinder* in the traditional way. Today in Palashpur there are only twenty-three adult *mahinders*. There are many child *mahinders* or *bagals*, however, especially from the Lohar caste.

Nagda System

When an untouchable man or a woman is hired on daily wage, it is called *nagda* labor. The wage ranges from five to ten rupees (i.e., 65 cents to $1.30) a day, depending on the season. A woman *nagda* is paid two rupees a day less than men. A *nagda* does manual labor of all kinds, for example house building, roofing, digging, and cultivation. When a Brahman or other high-caste man leases a parcel of land, he hires *nagda* to cultivate the land. The Brahman receives the entire produce from the land, but pays cash to the *nagda* cultivators for their work. He may pay rent for the land in cash or paddy. Many *nagda* laborers borrow money from the landowner and become bonded to work in his field (sometimes with less wage than the average). The landowner can thus maintain a pool of hired labor without entering into a permanent contract and obligation. The lending power of the landowners and the borrowing need of the landless poor create a cycle, leaving little choice for many cultivators but to seek jobs with high-caste landowners.

Kirshani System

In the *kirshani* system, the landowner supplies the cultivator with draft animals, a plow, fertilizer, seeds, and other cultivation needs, For his work, the *kirshan* receives one-third of the crop. Both the *kirshan* and his family work in the field. A *kirshan* can be trusted with a loan of money because he can pay back the loan with his produce.

Bhagchasi System

The *bhagchasi* cultivator supplies everything needed for cultivation, and both he and his family work the land. The landowner receives 55 percent of the paddy, or twenty-two "tins" (i.e., large kerosene cans) and the cultivator receives eighteen "tins" of paddy. A *bhagchasi* may engage a *nagda* laborer if necessary, and sometimes a *bhagchasi* and his family work in other fields as *nagda* themselves if they have spare time.

In addition to these four economic systems there is the *thika* system in which some untouchable cultivators engage. In the *thika* system, a fixed rent is paid to the landowner in the form of paddy, but the surplus crop belongs to the cultivator. In Palashpur, the village temple of Dharmaraj has some land dedicated to a deity, donated by the rich Zamindar family in the nearby village of Taltor.[3] The land belongs to the temple trust and is given on lease to the *thika* system.

Recent Changes in the Land Tenure System

The traditional power of the landowning castes over the landless untouchables has diminished gradually, since India's independence in 1947. In the past, landowners had omnipotent power over the landless peoples, and economic and social exploitation was sometimes excessive. Since independence, the government

3. Although the *zamindari* system has been abolished, this rich landowning family of Taltor is still referred to as Zamindar. The *zamindari* system in Palashpur is discussed later. The concept of *zamindari* is defined in the glossary.

has tried with partial success to enact several laws curtailing the rights of landowners. The present government of West Bengal, the Communist Party Marxist (CPM), is also eager to avoid oppression of the landless people and is encouraging a law enforcing the *bargadari* system. A *bargadar* cultivator was originally a landless *bhagchasi* or *kirshan* who worked in his *manib*'s fields in a hereditary way or over a very long period of time. A *bhagchasi* or *kirshan* of this caliber can now claim that the landowner cannot sell the land or transfer the cultivator's right to cultivate without his consent. If the *manib* does, he must share the sale price with the *bhagchasi* or *kirshan*. Palashpur landowners are now very careful to "keep good terms" with cultivators so that the latter do not take advantage of the new law. Some landowners are careful not to hire the same *bhagchasi* or *kirshan* over a long period of time in order to avoid the establishment of *bargadari* rights. There are at present twenty-two *bargadars* in Palashpur, of whom seven belong to the Baen caste. As lucrative as it sounds to the landless people, the *bargadari* system has many loopholes, and the economic condition of the untouchable cultivators has not changed much because of it. The new law has, however, created a great deal of tension, replacing traditional intercaste mutual trust. An illustration of this tension is provided by the case of a twenty-five-year-old *bargadar*, as recounted by a fellow Baen:

> Jagai Das is a *bhagchasi* with a Brahman *manib*. He wanted to *bargadar* his land but his *manib* became furious. Out of anger he dismissed him from his job contract as a *bhagchasi*. The poor man did not have any land to cultivate and looked for *nagda* work. But he could get only two months' work and earned only sixty rupees. When he could not find any job for days he took the help of the *upa-pradhan* (i.e., elected chief of the village administrative body). The *upa-pradhan* arranged his *bargadar* status. But when he took his plow to the field the *manib* came and beat him up. Jagai became very angry with his *manib*. He brought a lot of his own people, and the *manib* fled. Jagai plowed and transplanted the paddy. When the field was ready for harvest, Jagai asked the owner to accept his 55 percent share. The owner refused to have anything to do with Jagai, so Jagai sold the owner's share and deposited the money in the post-office savings account.

The government of West Bengal has instituted still another economic system called *pattadari.* Here the government reclaims land from rich landowners who usually live far from the village and who do not cultivate the land regularly. This "vested land" is distributed among landless men but not women in Palashpur. Such land belongs to the government, and the Department of Land Revenue receives a small rent from the cultivators. At present there are nine *pattadari* men in Palashpur, some with a meager one-third *bigha*. Even so, this is the first time in generations that men from these families have owned their own land.

Economic Activities of the Untouchable Castes

Untouchable males begin working with a plow at the age of twelve or thirteen, though they may start other agricultural pursuits earlier. These boys work for about seven or eight hours a day, either as a *mahinder* or a part-time herder of livestock. The youths are expected to clean the cow shed, prepare fodder, and feed the animals. These youths also provide the labor pool needed in high-caste homes. "No work, no food" one Lohar mother told her eight-year-old son.

A boy who is not a *mahinder* receives one rupee for each cow or buffalo he herds, and he receives twenty-five paise (one hundred paise equals one rupee) for each goat or sheep. The boy also receives three bowls of puffed rice a month (each bowl holds one kilogram of rice) and some jaggery (an unrefined brown sugar made from palm sap). These boys also receive a pair of shorts, a shirt, and a towel annually. Boys like ten-year-old Shyamal Lohar bring the money and puffed rice home to their mothers. One morning Shyamal brought his small bag of puffed rice to his mother, who poured it into the corner of her sari, making a tidy bundle. Touching her son's head and speaking to the anthropologist she beamed, "Look Didi [i.e., elder sister], my Shyamal is such a good boy. He works very hard to bring food for all of us." Shyamal looked happy but shy in front of the fieldworker.

A boy of ten can usually herd eight to ten head of cattle. Younger boys take care of goats and sheep. A boy can also have an "adopted" cow or "adopted" goat. In this system the boy must feed the cow but he receives the first calf and the first milk, after which he returns the cow to its original owner. The same system is followed for the goats, except that if the goat has two kids the boy takes one and the owner takes the other. Few boys are lucky enough, however, to have such "adopted" animals.

Most untouchable boys work all day. Only a few attend the local school, but those who do work both before and after school, and they often miss school during the growing season. Untouchable boys glean paddy, potatoes, and gather fruit or whatever other edibles they have access to. Many need to work on their own family's land received on contract from the owner. Children–including girls, as shown below–are often indispensable economic contributors to family subsistence in Palashpur, as they are throughout all of India and in a great many other locations worldwide (Arnold et al. 1975; Cook 1984; Nag, White, and Peet 1978).

Land and livestock are the most important areas of intercaste dependence in the economy of Palashpur, but intercaste cooperation is also necessary in other domains such as house building. Most of the houses in Palashpur are built by Lohar men, but high-caste people sometimes ask their *bhagchasi* or *kirshan* to build a house, and a *mahinder* may also help these builders, without extra pay. Hired laborers receive a daily wage of about five rupees. A *bhagchasi* or *kirshan* also gets one meal a day plus a rupee for palm wine. It takes about six weeks for one man to complete a ten-foot-square room with mud walls. Doors and windows are supplied by men of the Chhutor caste, and iron hinges are supplied by the Kamar. The roof is made by men of the Bauri caste living outside Palashpur. Nowadays, it costs about forty-five hundred rupees to build a small double-storied house with two ten-foot-square rooms downstairs and two upstairs. Thatch roofing is changed every five years, with annual repairs of fresh straw. A house also needs to be maintained by a regular plastering of "earth liquid" (i.e., a mixture of cow dung, straw, and mud), which is done by hired untouchable men or women, or a *mahinder.* The entryway and gates of richer homes are designed by a skilled Lohar mason, with carvings on cement plaster.

Men of the Chhutor and Kamar castes work together on wood and iron tools needed for agriculture and for the manufacture and repair of bullock carts. Both also supply household tools to the villagers. Date palm juice, palmyra palm juice, and jaggery are prepared by Lohar men and women for high-caste families who own the trees. The Sundi wine distiller depends mainly on expert untouchable men to prepare rice wine and palm wine.

As with untouchable males, untouchable females have a symbiotic relationship with the high castes, but without some of the basic privileges enjoyed by the men. Women throughout India form an indispensable labor force in the cultivation of rice. Rice, unlike wheat, needs teamwork. It is common during the rice-transplanting season to see women bending over the soil, working in a group. Even though men sometimes join the teamwork, women cultivators are known as "the rice transplanters." They start working at the age of ten or eleven, sometimes earlier. Men and women both agree that women sometimes work harder than men and that their output is often greater than that of men. Nonetheless they receive two rupees less than men for equal hours of work. Women also work with the men during weeding and harvesting. After harvesting the paddy, untouchable women boil and dry it in the homes of richer, high-caste villagers. Often a *bhagchasei* or *kirshan*'s wife or daughter performs these tasks at the landowner's home in order to repay an outstanding loan.

Women are not allowed to work with a plow, an implement reserved solely for males.[4] But during the rainy season, when the rice fields are flooded with an intermixture of water from the Kopai River, the irrigation canal, and the ponds, fishing in the rice fields becomes a profitable task for women and children. Women are allowed to use large round nets and fish traps to catch small fish from high-caste ponds. While men plow the land, women collect snails, conches, and fish for the family's daily meal. Any surplus is sold to high-caste households and to

4. This is very nearly a universal phenomenon found in societies such as those of traditional China, Southeast Asia, and South Asia. A taboo is almost always associated with women using this "prestigious" tool, but women enjoy more equal privileges in hoe cultivation, where a plow has no place. (See Ember 1983.)

passersby near the canal. Untouchable women also provide reserve labor for road building and house building within and outside the village. Moreover, they distill wine and palm juice to sell, and they supply brooms (Baen women) and baskets (Dom women), mats, and fans to high-caste homes.

Despite the considerable value of women's labor, women are excluded from the contractual *mahinder, bhagchasi,* and *kirshani* systems. They are ineligible for loans unless they have a husband or a son to stand as guarantor. Women of *bhagchasi* or *kirshani* families work in their family fields, but when their husbands die or abandon them (or when they are separated from their husbands for some other reason) they lose all rights to the land unless they have an adult son who can inherit the right after the father's death.

Many untouchable women work as domestics in high-caste homes. For their services they receive three to five rupees a month. The value of this payment is made clearer when one realizes that one kilogram of rice alone costs three-and-a-half rupees in Palashpur. A maid may also receive half a meal or her breakfast each day plus a new sari each year. She works at least six to seven hours a day—more on special occasions—washing, cleaning clothes and dishes, sweeping the courtyard, and helping in other odd jobs around the house. The salary of a domestic seems to have remained constant during the past twenty years. High-caste women do not mind doing this work so the demand for domestic services is slight unless the pay is very small.

Untouchable girls start helping their mothers from the age of five or six by collecting cow dung during the day to make fuel cakes; girls of seven or eight collect snails and fish, gleaned from the paddy fields, and gather potatoes and onions. They also collect twigs, leaves, and firewood for fuel. They mix cow dung and straw, and plaster this mixture as a round cake on a wall. After drying, these fuel cakes are collected and sold to high-caste homes. When a large number of cakes have been accumulated, women carry them on their heads to Santiniketan for selling. Girls from eight- to thirteen-years-of-age herd cows, buffaloes, and goats just as the boys do, and they are paid at the same rate. When untouchable girls get a little older they take jobs as domestics, just like their mothers. This is the time when adolescent girls start working in cultivation.

Untouchable girls in Palashpur seldom have time to play. But small groups of girls often roam around the village area, collecting mushrooms and greens from the edges of ponds, and collecting fuel, wood, twigs, and cow dung for home consumption and for sale. An untouchable family depends to a great extent on these girls for its daily protein, vegetable intake, and fuel. The girls also earn a bit of cash by selling these gathered commodities. Boys, too, help their families gather food—sometimes by stealing grain from the paddy fields. Indeed during the harvest season one frequently finds seven- and eight-year-old boys running through the fields at dusk with plastic bags full of paddy. Insofar as possible they hide themselves beneath the paddy plants. If the are caught they are slapped, but most of the time people ignore such petty theft. As helpful as this extra food is, parents generally agree that the girls are more attentive to the family's food needs than are boys.

The following cases show daily economic contributions made by untouchable girls to their families. One day in September, for example, eleven-year-old Milan Lohar supplied cows' milk to a high-caste home. For this daily activity she received seven rupees a month.[5] She also collected a large basket of cow dung, worth fifty paise, for fuel; she gathered a large *tal* fruit, which helped her family prepare bread for dinner (one *tal* is worth about seventy-five paise), and she gathered one medium-sized basket of greens worth about fifty paise. Two days later she collected a large basket of cow dung worth fifty paise, a medium basket of greens worth fifty paise, and a small basket of crabs and snails worth two rupees. The crabs and snails were to be used for both home consumption and for sale. Milan also herds ten cows and buffaloes every day for about six hours, and she cleans the cow shed and prepares the fodder. She does her food and fuel gathering before and after herding hours, which are approximately from ten o'clock in the morning to four o'clock in the afternoon.

5. Prices mentioned are based on the parent's assessment.

On a different September day, Juthika Lohar, another eleven-year-old girl, went fishing from seven o'clock to ten o'clock in the morning; her catch was intended for home consumption and for sale and was worth two rupees. She also collected a large basket of cow dung worth fifty paise, a small basket of mushrooms worth fifty paise, and a medium basket of greens. She collected twigs and firewood worth fifty paise for home consumption. Several days later, she sold cow dung fuel for seventy-five paise, collected fresh greens worth fifty paise for home use, and collected fresh greens worth fifty paise to be sold. She also caught crabs and fish worth one-and-one-half rupees for home consumption and sale. Juthika herds twelve cows and buffaloes. She too does her gathering before and after herding hours.

Santana Lohar's father described his ten-year-old daughter's weekly contribution to the family's "unseen income." He said, "Her mother and elder sister work all day at Santiniketan as maids. We wouldn't get much to eat if Santana was not there." According to her father's tabulation, Santana—the week before—provided fuel worth seventh-five paise for the daily cooking of lunch, tea, and dinner. She gathered fresh greens daily worth fifty paise; she collected cow dung daily worth fifty paise; she gleaned paddy and collected about half a kilogram a day for three weeks after the harvest. On one occasion she brought home some ripe mangoes, one large *tal* fruit, and green figs, and she collected a small basket of tamarind fruit for pickles. Moreover, she collected a small basket of jam fruits each day during its month-and-a-half season. She caught fish daily worth fifty paise, and she also collected snails three times, worth a total of one rupee. On two occasions she collected about a kilogram of potatoes and onions by gleaning. Finally, she once collected a small basket of *kachu,* a root vegetable.

The mother of ten-year-old Saraswati Hazra gave a similar accounting of her daughter's economic contribution to the family. Each day Saraswati collected fuel worth fifty paise. She also collected each day a basket of cow dung worth fifty paise, a medium basket of fresh greens worth thirty-five paise, and some snails worth fifty paise. Once she collected some tamarind worth seventy-five paise, and twice she collected mangoes worth seventy-five paise. Several times she collected dates and jam fruits. She caught fish almost daily worth fifty paise. Once she collected *tal,* and once she gathered mushrooms worth fifty paise. Finally, she collected potatoes and paddy on several occasions.

Some collecting—for example, the gathering of fuel (i.e., twigs, leaves, and firewood), the gathering of fish, snails, or greens, or the collection of cow dung—is done every day. The gathering of fruit or gleaning of paddy or potatoes, on the other hand, occurs only as appropriate occasions arise.

Girls are fully aware of their duties to their families. They also take pride and compete with one another slightly to see who can gather the most. Girls often play games while gathering food and fuel, but their games cannot lead them to neglect their work for they might be scolded, punished, or threatened with the deprivation of food if they do not finish their task.[6] Little girls accompany older girls in gathering, and they gradually learn the needed skills. Girls of nine, for example, usually recognize five different kinds of edible greens near the ponds and in the fields, and they can differentiate poisonous mushrooms from among four edible types. Children are often praised if they bring home crabs, snails, fish, or even a large *tal* fruit as a surprise. Most mothers show a sense of pride in telling about the girl's contribution to the family.

The Family as an Economic Team

In high-caste families, land is customarily owned by men, though Indian law today ensures equal rights of daughters to land. Traditional rules, however, hold strong in Palashpur in that only two high-caste women own land in their own names. Land is almost always handed down from father to sons, and despite the continuing reduction of available land over the years, the majority of the high-caste families still hold land jointly among the brothers. In a joint or extended family, a man with a salaried income is liable to contribute his income to the pool of money

6. Such threats are common in Palashpur, but rarely is a child deprived of food because of neglect of duties.

derived from the land. This income is especially important to meet dowry demands at the time of a daughter's or sister's marriage, to pay for a parent's funeral rites, or to pay for a feast at the time of a family crisis. Similarly, the dowry a man receives from his own marriage usually goes to the family to be used to enhance the family's status.[7]

Among the untouchables only four families—two Baen, one Lohar, and one Handi—own land, and this amounts to less than three *bighas* each. The entire family pools its income in untouchable families, and family members work together as a team in the rice fields. In spite of this collective effort most untouchable families complain about their deficit budget. Following are five cases of untouchable families struggling for survival as an economic team. The first three cases were described by men.

One sixty-year-old Baen man lives in a household with eight other family members. He works at Visva Bharati University as a part-time sweeper and earns 180 rupees a month. This is enough to buy one month's rice, oil, and salt for one person. His eldest son (age thirty-seven) is a *kirshan* with ten *bighas* of land, which he inherited from his father after the latter became too weak to work the land. The son, the son's wife and daughter (age twelve), the younger son (age thirty), and the younger son's wife all work the family fields. The eldest son has been able to purchase two *bighas* of land for himself but he has to hire *nagda* cultivators to work the land. This son receives one-third of the produce from the family field. The second son also works as a *nagda*, but in 1981 was able to get jobs for only two months. That year he earned only 180 rupees. The old man's granddaughter herds cows and buffaloes for two high-caste families. His wife and daughter-in-law are responsible primarily for their own domestic work and for work in the family field. Still, they sell cow dung cakes in Santiniketan when they can, and they sometimes work as *nagda* if a job is available. They catch fish during the rainy season to be used by the family. Other children in the

7. In a Hindu marriage ritual, the bride and her dowry are given as a gift to the groom, hence the wife's dowry and the wife herself are considered the husband's property. (See also Fruzzetti 1982; Goody and Tambiah 1973.) Matters such as these are amplified at considerable length later in this book.

family are too young to work. Even with everyone working, this family was unable to afford proper clothing or even full meals for the whole year.

The second household is headed by a thirty-five-year-old Lohar man with five family members. The man is a *kirshan*. He and his wife do all the work on ten *bighas* of land, for which they receive one-third of the produce. After working in the fields, both work as *nagda* for road building or in agriculture. The eldest son (an eleven-year-old) is a *mahinder*, and the younger son of nine attends Palashpur school. The daughter, also nine years old, cooks for the entire family during the agricultural season. She also gathers food and fuel for the family. She is enrolled at the night school but is often too tired after a day's work to attend. When there is no other work, the mother takes the responsibility for cooking.

The third family is headed by a forty-year-old Handi man who is a *kirshan* with eight *bighas* of land. He has no time for wage labor. His wife works as *nagda* after completing her work in the family field. During the weeding season the man has some spare time, so he temporarily works as a servant in his *manib*'s household. There he helps with the roofing and plastering, and he sometimes helps build a needed extra room. For this he receives a meal and one rupee daily. The paddy he receives after harvest is not enough to last him the year. His daughter (age fifteen) works in the field and as a domestic for three rupees a month, and his son (age ten) herds cows. The family barely manages to get the food they need, and they always need more money for clothing.

The following two accounts concerning the economic life of untouchable families were given by women. As described by a twenty-two-year-old Lohar woman,

> I worked for twenty days in July–August [the month of Shravana], and I received about one hundred rupees cash, but I spent all the money on food. I had no work during the middle of August to the middle of September [Bhadra-Aswin]. I caught fish and snails, and earned only about twenty rupees. I spent it all—and stayed hungry all the time. Whenever we found a *tal* we would just suck it or make bread with it. We had a little rice one day. From the end

> of September into October [during the month of Kartik] I gleaned paddy and sold cow dung fuel. It was not until the harvest time [November–December] that I found a job in the field and earned about seventy-five rupees. I bought a sari for twenty-five rupees at that time. In the summer I got a job digging for road construction and I paid back some of our debt.

This woman, who was pregnant and married to a *nagda* cultivator, never mentioned her husband's income, perhaps because his income was so meager that it provided only for his own food. When asked about other sources of food, she replied, "I gather greens, collect snails or conches, or anything edible from the pond or bush. That is why I can still work with so little rice."

The next case was given by a twenty-five-year-old Handi woman:

> I worked during July–August [in Shravana] for twenty days and earned seventy-five rupees, and I did five days' extra work for thirty rupees. I saved thirty rupees and spent the rest on food during August–September [Bhadra-Aswin]. In September–October [Aswin] I could not find a job. I gleaned some paddy, and I worked during the harvest and received one hundred rupees. I spent thirty rupees to buy a new sari, and also paid back the loan my husband took from his *manib*. During the four months in spring and summer my husband's salary [given in paddy and a little cash] fed me. Once in a while I got a digging job, and I earned some money by selling fish. Now I have a baby and it is very hard to go for *nagda* work.

This woman's husband is a *mahinder.* She is fortunate enough to receive at least one full meal a day because her husband's dinner is usually large enough for two. Neither of these women was able to keep any cash savings, and they often had to borrow from high-caste homes. Women from the *bhagchasi* and *kirshan* families have the same work patterns as described above but they have a supply of paddy from the family land, which partially fulfills their need for family food.

High-caste women depend entirely on their husbands for their livelihood. This fact is symbolized in high-caste Hindu marriage ritual when the husband offers his new bride a plate of rice and a sari, saying, "I promise to give you food and clothing for the rest of your life." Untouchable women stand in sharp contrast to high-caste women, as revealed in a rhyme learned early by untouchable girls:

> Bhat deina bhatare
> Bhat dei gatare.

Liberally translated, this rhyme means "your husband does not give you rice; you get rice through your own strength (or body)."

CHAPTER 3

Village Social Organization

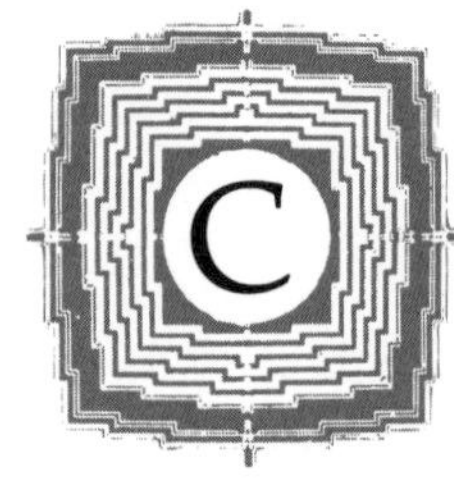

ommunity life in Palashpur is influenced to a large degree by caste membership. An individual's birth into a given caste provides his or her identity within a social group, and this in turn relates the individual to the rest of the community. Kakar (1978, 122–23) describes the significance of castes as follows:

> Usually, a jati [caste] or member participates in one of the jati's several traditional occupations, and his [marriage] partner will almost certainly belong to his jati. His friendship with other jati members tends to be closer than those with persons of other jatis with whom his relations are more formal, governed as they are by unwritten codes prescribing and proscribing relationships between jatis. Although some families of a particular jati may live in the same village, the jati extends beyond the confines of any single village.

Although castes of Palashpur do not necessarily follow their hereditary occupations, there is a cleavage between two large social groups, the *chhotolok* (i.e., illiterate, "uncivilized" people) or *chhotojat* (i.e., "inferior" caste), on the one hand, and *bhadralok* (i.e., literate, "civilized" people) or *barojat* (i.e., "superior" caste) on the other. One who performs manual labor is almost invariably associated with *chhotolok.* This includes the four castes at the bottom of the caste structure, as described in chapter 2. They are lumped together as "untouchables," though they are themselves stratified into several subgroups. The Chhutor, Kamar, and Napit men, who belong to the lower strata of the high-caste grouping, till their own land and are also called *chhotolok.* Chhutor and Kamar women also work on their family land, but they follow other caste rules identified with the high-caste portion of the community.

The term *bhadrolok* is also associated with the literacy level of a caste. A Brahman may refer to any other caste—for example, a Kayastha or Satgop—as *chhotojat,* but the latter castes would not be called *chhotolok.* On the other hand, an illiterate Brahman can be called *barojat,* but not a *bhadralok.* Generally, however, all high-caste men—excepting those in the lower strata (unless they have received some formal schooling)—are called *bhadralok* in Palashpur. The term *barojat* is a relative term and depends on the position of a person's caste in relation to others. Moreover, when a lower-level high-caste or untouchable man becomes formally educated (e.g., goes to college) or acquires other symbols of *bhadralok* life-style—such as polished manners and speech, and clean clothing—he may be called *bhadralok,* though some high-caste individuals resent this usage.

Schooling in Palashpur

In Palashpur, most high-caste men know how to read and write. This may not be true, however, for older high-caste women. In the local school, attended by children from Palashpur as well as from surrounding villages, students of both sexes come mainly from the high castes, although the number of untouchable schoolchildren is gradually increasing. At present no untouchable child goes to school beyond Class III (about age twelve). Among the high castes, on the other hand, fourteen men and two women graduated from college, and ten men and one woman now attend college.

In comparison to the high-caste literacy level, the level of literacy among untouchables is very low. Within the untouchable portion of the community only three students have studied Class VIII (finishing junior high at the local school). Among the Baen, six boys and four girls (all from one family) attend school up to Class III; three men among the Handi have attended school, but no one from the Dom families attends school. Palashpur also has a night school for untouchable children, where thirty children–mostly girls–are enrolled. On the average, ten of these children attend school on any given night.

Intracaste and Intercaste Relations

Members of the various high castes disagree about the correct ranking of castes in Palashpur. There seems to be general agreement, however, that the Kayastha and Satgop are directly beneath Brahmans in the status hierarchy. Brahmans take water from Kayastha and Satgop, and the Kayastha and Satgop take water from the Banik, Tabuli, and Napit only. The Sakaro, Sundi, Kaivarta, Chhutor, and Kamar take water from each other but not from the untouchables. A person's caste is often referred to as whether it is *jalchal* (i.e., a person from whom one may accept water). High castes must also follow certain food taboos regarding the use of meat, chicken, and eggs. High-caste persons may eat goat meat or mutton, but they may not eat pork or beef. Currently, no untouchable or high-caste person within the village eats beef, but some high-caste men are known to have eaten chicken outside the village, and chicken eggs are becoming popular. Moreover, high-caste men may indulge in liquor (an act tolerated but looked upon as improper) in the liquor shop, though strictly in male company. High-caste women never touch wine, but both untouchable men and women drink heavily during weddings and other festivals. Untouchable children are also given palm wine, which is believed to make them strong.

Brahmans do not allow anyone to touch their cooking pot. Hence, for a picnic or feast the cook is always hired from the Brahman caste. At one point an effort was made to integrate castes at school feasts, but it met with strong resistance. High-caste children were allowed to cut the vegetables, but only Kayastha and Satgop were allowed to fetch water. Untouchable children were not allowed to come near the cooking area lest they should inadvertently touch something. The serving of guests during wedding feasts at the home of Brahmans shows three broad divisions of castes: Brahmans are fed first, followed by the Sudra, (i.e., the non-Brahman high castes grouped together); high-caste women are served after men and children. Untouchable men, women, and children are served last. Whereas the high-caste guests are served on the porch or inside the house, untouchables are served in the courtyard.

Each caste has several subgroups that may be arranged hierarchically.[1] In Palashpur a Brahman of the highest rank belongs to the Kulin group, with family names of Mukherjea (Mukhapadhyya), Banerjea (Bandopaddhayya), and Chatterjea (Chattapaddhayya). Families of the priestly class, Bhattacharyya, hold a lower rank. The Bhattacharyya Brahman performs priestly service for high-caste families only. An eighty-year-old Chattapaddhayya Brahman said, "In our youth a Bhattacharyya Brahman used to perform only for the Brahmans and two other high castes. Now they perform for the *naba sakha* group." *Naba sakha*, he explained, means a guild of nine castes with hereditary occupations of Chitey (sweet makers), Pitey (potters), Kamar (ironsmiths), Gopa (cow herders/milk sellers), Napit (barbers), Gochali (betel-leaf traders), and Malakar (those who work with fresh flowers and "pith" flowers, the latter being floral designs carved or woven from the spongy pith taken from reeds that grow in West Bengal). He continued, "In the past, the Banik or Bene were not included in this group—now they have been accepted." Not all groups of the *naba sakha* live in Palashpur. If a Bhattacharyya Brahman is not available to perform priestly services, Brahmans of lower rank (e.g., Chahravarty and Adhikari, both belonging outside the village) officiate for the high castes of lower rank—for example, the Kamar, Chhutor, Kaivarta, and Sundi.

The Lohar are the highest ranking untouchable caste. They are also divided into four subgroups—Lohar, Bagdi, Meyte, and Mal or Rajbanshi. During the festival of Dharmapuja—the wor-

1. The largest number of subgroups was found among the Kayastha. There were seventy-two subgroups arranged into two main groups, namely, Kulin and Moulik.

ship of the village diety—a Satgop priest performs the necessary rituals in Lohar, Dom, and Handi homes. Sometimes a Chahravarty Brahman can be hired for a Lohar marriage. The Dom are subdivided into three groups, the Akurey (highest rank), Bagjiney (drummer or dancer), and Gheso (basket maker). The Handi have three subdivisions, namely, Mahato or Baro Hazra (the priestly class with high status), Samprey (one who works with leather), and Dari (whose women work as midwives). The Mahato is also called Handi-Brahman within the Handi caste. The Baen's four subgroups are Roitan (those who play *dhak,* the very large drum), Khota (those who play *madal,* the small drum), Chamar (those who work with cowhide), and Ariye (those who work with cane and bamboo as basket makers). Of all the untouchables, the Baen are lowest ranking. Although men of other untouchable castes may drink and dine with Baen, women and children do not share rice with them. If children accept food from the Baen, they must take a *doob,* that is, a ritual cleansing of the body, by submerging themselves in the water of a pond or river.

Caste norms are frequently violated in day-to-day social interaction. For example, when asked, "Does a Chahravarty Brahman officiate for a Dom or a Handi?" a young Dom man answered, "Any Brahman would come if we pay him." Such comments are significant in the present-day rural scene where financial pressures often override traditional caste prejudice. Even the most dominant caste group, the Kulin Brahman—where caste discrimination and rigidity has been most profound—has had to accommodate to the pressure of change and drastic events within the community. Nonetheless, there is a tendency to return again to the traditional ways after the pressure has been relieved. Even though the ritual superiority of the Brahman remains unchanged, the traditional power of the Brahmans as the dominant caste is being curtailed today in secular spheres, especially in politics and economics. In the Indian census record, for example, castes are not recognized except as "scheduled castes." ("Scheduled castes" refers primarily to the untouchables but also includes some of the lowest echelon high castes.) The scheduled castes are given special privileges by the government regarding job facilities, admission to medical and engineering schools, stipends, land, and so forth.

Caste in the Political Structure

In an earlier chapter we mentioned the government's recent acts that have brought about numerous changes in the role of landowners within rural communities. The change in the attitude of the government toward the landless untouchables has also brought a great change in the village political structure. In the past, Palashpur was ruled by the Brahmans, while the untouchables were powerless. In the past the village also had a political body called *dharam sarkar* (an office or political body associated with the principle deity of the village, Dharmaraj), which consisted only of Brahmans. Traditionally, this political body dealt with divorce, land disputes, rape, adultery, and other civil offenses. Only very severe offenses such as murder were sent to the urban court. The villagers were summoned to the body by announcements and drumbeat, and they were allowed to witness the legal proceedings. The body could fine or ostracize a person from the village, and any fine was taken as a contribution to the Dharmaraj fund. This political body existed at the time of national independence in 1947, but it gradually lost its power to a formal governing body that worked under the district and state administration, called *gram panchayat.*

Since the time of national independence an awareness of the oppression of the landless portion of the community has grown. The present Communist Party Marxist (CPM) government policy has tried to generate mass consciousness about class distinction. The untouchable castes are now politically united to secure their rights, especially in land distribution. Palashpur villagers represent voters from two parties, the CPM and the Congress I (Indira Congress). During the last election, the CPM committee at Palashpur—consisting of both high and untouchable castes—suggested electing an untouchable as the representative of the village on the *gram sabha,* that is, on the village administrative body that oversees ten villages including Palashpur (and named Palashpur *gram sabha*). Palashpur *gram sabha* is under Ruppur *gram panchayat,* which is a larger body of *gram sabha* representatives from five *gram sabhas.* There are twelve hundred voters for the Palashpur *gram sabhas,* of which 25 percent are from scheduled castes, 15 percent from scheduled tribes, and 60 percent from higher castes. A Baen from Palashpur (belonging to the lowest rank of the untouchable sector of the community) was elected as *upa-pradhans,* that is, representative to the *gram sabha.* In 1983 this man went on to be elected the *pradhan,* or chief representative of twelve *gram sabhas. Upa-pradhans* from different *gram sabhas* work under one *pradhan* of the *panchayat.* The *upa-pradhan* acts as the head of the constituent villages to collect revenues and to oversee land disputes and conflicts of the local people. The high-caste sector of the community has accepted the Baen leader without apparent grudge. However an old, disgruntled Brahman—a man who had previously been a leading member of *dharam sarkar*—said about the untouchables, "we cannot avoid the trend of time. Scheduled castes are all illiterates and drunkards. They cannot accept responsibility. That is why we did not include them in the committee. They had no desire to be included. Why are they coming now? Because the government is doing it. The party [CPM] came, and the question of caste vanished."

Three high-caste men sought election as independent candidates. Despite their defeat, members of opposing parties are not hostile. The untouchable leader, a thirty-eight-year-old Baen man, now sits with the Brahmans in political discussions and in the tea shops, but the caste barrier is unbroken during socio-religious functions. The political arena remains secular and basically untouched by caste considerations.

Now there is a strong sense of caste consciousness among landless members of the community, who are gradually coalescing into a viable political power-group. To an outsider the Palashpur untouchables seldom refer to themselves as belonging to a particular caste, rather they refer to themselves as "We, the poor *chhotolok*" (i.e., the "inferior" people). The high-caste community also refers to them in this way. For example, a seventy-five-year-old Chatterjea Brahman commented, "Previously the *chhotoloks* bowed to us whenever they wanted to speak to us. Now they stand straight, as if they were our equals or even superiors." On another occasion, when our female Lohar research assistant walked with one of the authors, Chaki-Sircar, through the village, in neat clothing and a small notebook in her hand, she heard a sarcastic remark behind her: "Look, soon there will be no distinction between *chhotolok* and *bhadrolok*." A common expression among high-caste adults to their misbehaving children is, "Don't behave like the children of *chhotolok*," and a frequently heard abuse among the high caste is, "Son of a *chhotolok*!"

Caste, Kinship and the Family

Kinship and Caste

Villagers marry within their own caste group, though spouses rarely come from the village itself. Kinship is reckoned patrilineally, through the male line, and brides generally live with their husbands in or near the household of the husband's father—though three couples in the village (two Brahman and one Baen) live with the family of the bride. Wives of Palashpur come from eighty-six different villages and towns, most within a thirty-mile radius, and the daughters of Palashpur have been married to men from eighty-seven different places outside Palashpur. Village exogamy is not a strict rule, but it is expected because villagers do not want their daughters-in-law to be too close to their natural kin. In the last ten years, however, youths from within the village have married one another. These are called "love" marriages.

Villagers have a wide network of kin relationships which become especially apparent during family rituals such as weddings, funerals, religious festivals, and *upanayana* (the "sacred thread" or puberty rite of a Brahman adolescent boy). During family rituals it is most important to invite one's close kin, but if budget permits, one's distant kin are invited too. Important family rituals are not limited to the immediate family. Weddings, for example, establish ties between two families, and accordingly kin should be present to support this union. Kin's contribution is necessary in funeral feasts too. Reciprocity of obligations and exchange of gifts play an important part in these relationships. During a daughter's wedding in high-caste families, for example, close kin are expected to contribute to the dowry, but this dowry should be reciprocated when the other's turn comes.

During certain festivals such as Dharmapuja—the festival of the village deity, in April—most of the villagers expect their kinsmen to visit and join the festival. The crowd of relatives is most visible in Baen households, because two hundred to five hundred Baen drummers from many villages come to attend the festival and perform for the deity, Dharma. Professional drummers play free of charge for Charmaraj as a dedication to the deity. The festival does not start until the Baen from the Sukhbazaar area come to offer their homage. Thus, Baen kinsmen from a large area have an annual caste congregation during the festival week. On this occasion Baens find new work assignments, negotiate children's marriages, and resolve family conflicts.

Kinship and Marriage

Social relationships among affinal kin are asymmetrical in that a woman's family holds an inferior status to her husband's family (Fruzzetti 1982). Such inequalities of relationship are overt in high-caste marriages.

Most marriages in Palashpur are arranged by parents and other close kinsmen. Elders of the two families negotiate with each other, discussing family genealogies and matching horoscopes of the prospective bride and groom. In high-caste marriages the couple must belong to the same subgroup of a caste but they must come from different clans or *gotras.* There are seven *gotras* for each high caste. During the wedding a bride is ritually transferred from her *gotra* to her husband's. Prior to marriage it is customary for the prospective groom to come with some of his close friends to "look at" the girl. Of course the young man also faces many critical eyes that, in like manner, examine his appearance and his behavior. However, if he has a job or considerable property or land, his looks are seldom brought into question.[2] If the girl passes the beauty test, elders from the boy's family sometimes ask the girl to walk, in order to scrutinize any possible deformity. If all goes well, the elders

2. Quite often women relatives of the young man come to "look at" the girl and make a final decision. Sometimes young men also accompany their mothers or sisters to "look at" the girl.

negotiate the dowry transaction. To families of young marriageable daughters in Palashpur, dowry is often a cruel reality.

Dowry and the Liability of Daughters

Being a patrilineal society under the influence of the Brahmanic patriarchy, there is a strong emphasis in Palashpur on having male children for the perpetuation of the lineage and for old age security. As noted above, in marriage relationships the girl's family has a diminished status. The liability of a daughter is further aggravated by the custom of dowry. In Palashpur many high-caste families have to sell land or borrow money in order to pay for their daughter's marriage. The average dowry is worth about eight thousand rupees in cash, plus gold jewelry for the girl, payment of the wedding expenses for the groom's family (especially the wedding feast), and sometimes gifts to the groom's family of bicycles, transistor radios, wristwatches, and clothing. The cost can go much higher if grooms are college graduates with salaried jobs and family land. In high-caste weddings the groom's family sends a long list of gifts (usually the number of men's *dhotis* and women's saris are mentioned) to be given by the bride's family to the groom's relatives. The groom's party, called *barjatri,* joins the girl's family feast. The number of people in these *barjatri* varies from 10 to 150. Sometimes the *barjatri* arrives in rented public buses hired at the expense of the girl's family. These people expect to be treated as most honored guests. These "honored guests" traditionally behave in intrusively demanding and impolite ways, which is tolerated with expected humility. When the girl departs from her natal family after her wedding, she departs with a big share of the family fortune—without any obligation of reciprocity. After her wedding the girl belongs to her husband's family, and she loses all rights in her father's home. She is now expected to visit her parents' home only as a welcomed guest. The length and frequency of her visits are controlled by the elders of her husband's family, and these people often ignore the emotional content of her relationship with her parents. Hence, the sojourn of a newly married woman to her husband's home is often associated with a painful emotional experience. The bride, her mother, sisters, friends, and little girls cry sadly. Often the brothers and the father also sob with a feeling of personal loss. Following a marriage ritual in Palashpur, it is common to see a large crowd of women villagers crying as they watch a daughter of the village leave.

The dowry in high-caste marriages is seldom considered a gift to the bride. In fact, in a Brahmanic marriage the bride herself is ritually given as a virginal gift to the groom, along with her dowry (see also Bennett 1983; Fruzzetti 1982; Roy 1975).[3] Ideologically, then, the bride and her dowry become the groom's possessions. Sometimes the groom's family does not trust the girl's father to purchase the dowry gifts of jewelry, furniture, clothing, utensils, and the like. Rather, the groom's family demands cash to buy the gifts themselves. This asymmetrical kin relationship continues long after the daughter's marriage, and the daughter's family must continue to send gifts on ritual occasions, without reciprocity from the son-in-law's family. Because of the economic hardship imposed by this cultural ideology, Palashpur has numerous spinsters, and many villagers fear there will be more in the future.[4]

Until five years ago the untouchable portion of the community in Palashpur had not adopted the high-caste custom of dowry. Instead, the girl's family received gifts from the groom's family as compensation for the loss of an economically productive family member. These gifts were returned to the groom's family if the marriage did not work. Over the last few years, however, Palashpur untouchables have begun to imitate the high castes in demanding cash from the bride's family. The custom is now becoming pervasive. People often borrow money for their daughter's marriage or sell their meager belongings to meet the expense. But if the girl returns to her parents after her marriage, her family often demands the dowry back.

On the average, untouchable girls marry when they are around fifteen or sixteen years old; untouchable men tend to

3. Indian law currently prohibits a person from taking dowry, but the law is ignored throughout much of India.

4. A "spinster" in Palashpur is an unmarried woman over thirty or thirty-five. Currently there are five spinsters in the village, but some fear there will be twenty women whose families cannot provide dowries in the next ten years.

marry when they are twenty or twenty-one. Most marriages are arranged by parents, though "love marriages" are common for second marriages. When a man remarries, the marriage ceremony is performed by a priest, if the bride has never before been married. But if the woman has been married before, her remarriage is not performed by a priest, even if her husband is marrying for the first time. The second marriage of a woman (called *sanga*)—whether she is a divorcee, a widow, or an unwed mother—is simple. Men and women from both families gather, and after a simple ritual involving the exchange of flower garlands and the husband putting *sindur* on the woman's forehead, the couple are pronounced man and wife.

Separation and Divorce

Untouchable marriages differ from high-caste marriages in at least one critical way. High-caste marriages are indissoluble, but two high-caste women in the village are separated from their husbands.[5] These women continue to wear vermillion powder (the *sindur*) in the part of their hair, a dot on their forehead, and iron or conch shell bangles, all of which symbolize their status as married women. In Palashpur, the social ethic of the marital bond is predetermined and sacred; it is so strong that high-caste women are expected to continue living with their husbands even in the most miserable of marriages. High-caste women's economic insecurity along with their lack of rights in their own fathers' homes make their social position as a divorcee extremely vulnerable. "If our husbands beat us to death, we have no way out," said one high-caste woman of fifty-five. She continued, "We just pray that our daughters will be in good homes." A wife's natal family should not interfere in the girl's marital relationship; neither should they encourage the girl to return to her father, for she would then be an economic burden. The family's reputation would also suffer because of the "bad example" set by the daughter. Indeed, the girl's relatives are even discouraged from visiting

5. Postindependence law allows divorce on the grounds of mutual incompatibility. But so far there have been no divorces in the high-caste sector of the community.

her too often. However, if the daughter is treated badly, the kin relationship between the two sets of families is damaged and her husband's family may acquire an ill reputation within their caste—which could lead to their having trouble finding suitable matches for their other children. A domineering mother-in-law is somewhat accepted, but if she becomes too overbearing people might brand her "a woman who tortures her daughter-in-law." Such public censure helps create safeguards for women to some degree. Nonetheless, there are at least eleven high-caste homes in Palashpur where wives have been beaten by their husbands, often at the instigation of the wives' mothers-in-law.

An untouchable husband does not face the same responsibility of taking care of his wife and children. He can abandon them or drive his wife out of the household if he finds her incompatible. Similarly, untouchable women may leave their husbands. Little social stigma is attached, and no one seeks outside legal assistance. The wife simply returns to her father's home if he is nearby. Otherwise she asks her male kinsmen to fetch her. These men then confront her in-laws and demand the daughter back. This is apt to lead to considerable verbal abuse and sometimes to physical fights, especially if the dowry is demanded back.[6] When two parties come to a mutual agreement for separation, the girl's father asks for a written statement attesting to the end of the marriage. After they leave their husbands, these untouchable women usually live with their fathers until they remarry. Common reasons given in the village for separation include, "He gets drunk and beats her," "She did not like him at all," and "They did not give her good food and clothing."

Among the Baen of Palashpur there are nine women and five men (ages twenty-two to fifty) who have been married at least twice. One twenty-five-year-old woman has been married four times, and a man of forty has been married five times. In thirty-two Lohar families we found seventeen men and sixteen women between the ages of twenty to fifty who have been married more than once. One Dom man married twice, and a woman just

6. Traditionally, dowry among the untouchables consisted of five gifts: a sari and four utensils. Some fathers also offered a cow or a goat. Nowadays the girl's dowry includes an additional gift of cash to the groom.

recently left her husband. Moreover, during the course of fieldwork for this volume, one fifteen-year-old Lohar girl and one sixteen-year-old Baen girl refused to go back to their husbands after returning to their fathers. Both families tried hard to convince the girls to return, but both girls said, "I don't like him. I won't go." In one case, when the young husband came to fetch his wife, the girl yelled at him in public, "If you come again I'll throw stones at you and break your head." This kind of independent behavior is unheard of among high-caste wives and is often referred to by them as "*chhotolok*'s behavior." The Baen girl was later readmitted into the local school, and the Lohar girl simply went back to her former life-style as a cultivator and domestic servant. The families of these girls do not express any shame about their daughters' behavior, but they worry about the girls' remarriage. Untouchable women with grown children seldom break their marriages, but many leave their husbands to live with their natal relatives for considerable periods of time.

Widowhood and Remarriage

Among high-caste women there is no tradition of remarriage for a widow but a high-caste man may, if he wishes, remarry after his wife's death. High-caste widows, no matter how young, must follow strict dietary rules of vegetarianism, and they must fast at the time of a full moon, a new moon, and on every eleventh day following a full moon and a new moon (often without drinking water). They must wear all-white saris, and they must lead an altogether austere, celibate life. They must forsake all cosmetics and all symbols of marriage such as *sindur,* conch shell bangles, iron bangles, and preferably all other jewelry. In fact, a proper widow should appear to be an asexual person. Widows without children often return to live with their parents' families, but a widow with children continues to live in her husband's extended family. Widowhood of a high-caste woman may be described as "social death" (Chaki-Sircar 1980), hence the presence of widows is avoided on auspicious occasions such as weddings. In contrast, a married woman dressed in bright colors—especially wearing *sindur,* jewelry, and a sari with a bright red border—is considered to be like Laxmi, the goddess of grace and prosperity.

Her marriage symbols of *sindur* and conch shell bangles are considered sacred, bestowing inherent power to the woman (Fruzzetti 1982; Roy 1975). A devout high-caste widow is considered a ritually superior person. Her self-abnegation endows her ideologically with a spiritual power of wifely devotion to the dead husband.[7] In real life, however, widowhood is the least desired state in the life-cycle of high-caste women (Harper 1969).

A short case study illustrates some of the problems of widowhood in Palashpur. A beautiful Satgop woman of fifty-five wore an all white sari, with her knee-length black hair bundled casually into a bun. She had become a widow at the age of eleven. She said,

> I don't even recall my husband's face. I didn't realize what a terrible thing happened to me when my husband died. My parents brought me back to live with them, but later my elder sister brought me here to live in Palashpur with her. She gave up her nonvegetarian diet for me—even though her husband was alive—because she could not stand to eat "good" food without giving me some. When I became a young woman I gradually realized how deprived I was of everything. I wanted to attend school but I was not allowed. People said I was too beautiful and should be protected from outside life. My family was afraid that I might become morally loose. I know a Hindu widow can be married legally, but nobody cares for justice when it concerns women.[8]

Satgop widows in other Satgop-dominated villages near Palashpur do not follow such severe rules of austerity. Only Brahman and Kayastha widows are subjected to such suffering. But the

7. The Hindu concept of *shakti* refers to the spiritual energy of women, often associated with their power of self-abnegation and suffering. The extreme expression of this belief seems once to have been the ideological basis for the custom of "widow burning" or *sati* (Chaki-Sircar 1980). This form of suicide was looked upon as the greatest expression of self-sacrifice a woman could make to honor her dead husband. The suffering of present-day widows is the legacy of *sati*, but instead of physical death, women have now accepted "social death" (see Chaki-Sircar 1980).

8. A law allowing remarriage of high-caste widows was passed in 1857. This was a result of a prolonged battle between the nineteenth-century social reformer Vidyasagar and the orthodox Brahman society. Vidyasagar, himself a renowned Sanskrit scholar, cited ancient Hindu codes to justify the remarriage of high-caste widows.

Satgop minority in Palashpur follows the dominant Brahman model to justify their high status in the caste hierarchy.

Other women of Palashpur also complain of social injustice associated with their gender, as is shown by the following case of a twenty-nine-year-old Brahman widow with a six-year-old son:

> I don't see any reason why a woman must suffer. I was my husband's third wife. He was my father's age. I was forced to marry him because he did not ask for a dowry. My father was poor and he did not want to miss this opportunity. My husband used to get drunk and beat me up. I hated him. He even suspected that the baby was not our own. He was a miserable person. I suffered so much–I wished him dead. He died after five years. Now I have to live like this. I have no education to earn a living. My step-daughter liked me since the time I first came here. She is a very loving girl. Now she takes care of me.

Seven other high-caste widows in their twenties to sixties also felt that it was a social injustice to be treated so harshly, but none of them believed a woman should remarry if she has a child–because the child must belong to the father's lineage. If a high-caste mother does remarry, she must give up her children.

Untouchable women do not follow the Brahmanic model of widowhood. Young widows' remarriages by *sanga* are sometimes arranged by their families. Moreover, love marriages are frequent. That is, the couple has a romantic relationship, and their families ultimately arrange *sanga*. However, untouchable bachelors rarely marry a widow or a divorcee.

Deviations from Traditional Marital Standards

During the past decade there have been several love marriages in high-caste families. Such events are tolerated only if both partners belong to the same subgroup of a caste, and even then only after a great struggle against the elders. Otherwise, the couple may be ostracized from the community. In marriages between partners of the same caste, the girl's family may object only if they do not think the groom is suitable. In spite of the dowry pressure, high-caste families work hard "to settle" their daughters or sisters with good husbands. People also take pride in their daughter's or sister's husband. The young man's family feels cheated because in a love marriage one cannot demand an extravagant dowry. Moreover, the young woman is a member of the community and has been known to the family since childhood. Her in-laws cannot treat her too strictly lest their neighbors and her parents become sympathetic toward her.

Some families concede to a love marriage following an extended tug-of-war between sons and elders. Some families, however, succeed in convincing one of the lovers to give up the idea of a love marriage. Sometimes the boy is lured by the prospect of a dowry, and he drops the girl to marry another chosen by his elders. In other cases, however, the couple in love move to a nearby town and marry there under civil law. For instance, one couple left the village early in the morning, and, with the help of the girl's maternal uncle, got married under civil law. The girl put a vermillion dot on her forehead and parted her hair, wore a conch shell bangle and stood in the temple yard of Dharmaraj deity. While she waited there bashfully, keeping her eyes on the ground and surrounded by curious children, the young man went to see his parents. The news had already reached his family, who became verbally abusive about the girl's family and scolded the young man for his irresponsible behavior. Elderly neighbors overheard the ruckus and came in saying, "These young people have made a mistake. But after all, the girl is very pretty and comes from a Kulin Brahman home. He did not go for a low-caste girl. Forgive them and accept the bride as the Laxmi of your household."

When the mother of the boy gave her consent, other women went to the temple yard and held the bride gently by the hand. They blew conch shells and ululated while bringing the girl into the home of her husband-to-be.[9] The bride's family was conspicuously absent from the scene. Within six months, however, the girl left her husband's home and returned to her parents because she did not get along with her mother-in-law. Her husband continued living with his parents, but spent nights with his

9. Ululation, along with blowing of a conch shell, is associated with an auspicious event, for example the birth of a child, a wedding, or a worship. It is always performed by women.

wife. He helped at his father-in-law's tea shop, often running the tea shop with his wife. The other five cases of love marriage in Palashpur were not associated with such family tension.

The most shocking event in Palashpur occurs when young high-caste youths marry untouchables. This has happened on three occasions. On one, a young Brahman man with a college degree married a Dom girl. It happened again when a high-caste Chhutor girl married an untouchable Dhopa from another village, and again when a Brahman girl married a Muslim teacher from outside the village. All of these involved civil marriages, and in no case did the couple return to the village to live. However, the Brahman youth—after three years of marriage—now returns occasionally to visit his mother. His father still refuses to talk to him.

About twenty-five years ago, a nineteen-year-old Chhutor woman became pregnant by a twenty-four-year-old Brahman lover. In those days youth from different caste groups could not think of marriage. The baby was born, and the Brahman father gave money to support it. Although the Brahman eventually got married to a Brahman woman and had a family, the Chhutor woman never married. She has lived all her life at her parents' home. Her daughter, however, was married in due course. People sympathized with her because "she was a nice girl and never even had an affair with another man."[10] A fifty-five-year-old Brahman man said of this affair, "If it happened now, the couple would have been married."

Despite strong social control over the moral behavior of high-caste girls in Palashpur, four cases are talked about where girls defied the rules of "morality." One woman refused to live with her husband and is now having an affair with a married man within the village. Another young woman continues to have affairs with men both from the village and outside. Villagers gossip maliciously about her. Whenever a groom's party comes to "look at" her, some of the villagers make sure that they know about the girl's "character." Two of these women are daughters of widows who have no means of providing dowry; the other

10. Here again, a woman's self-abnegation is regarded as an expression of her spiritual superiority.

appears to be a social rebel, for she makes no secret of her adventures with men and, in fact, sometimes displays her affection for men in public—a reprehensible act by conventional standards. Recently she went out with a Santal tribesman from an adjacent village. The two went to a movie at Bolpur, but after the late movie she did not return home. Villagers thought they had eloped but the next morning the girl came back. It was the day of her younger brother's *upanayana,* and the house was filled with guests for the community feast. A high-caste young man commented, "She does this not only to disobey her parents but to defy everything the society stands for." Her case seems to be one possible expression of rebellion by some marriageable unmarried daughters of Palashpur. Nonetheless, techniques of social control are powerful enough to keep the majority of unmarried women sexually uninvolved until after marriage.

Moral Behavior of High-Caste Men and Intercaste Tension

As in the case of women, an "ideal" man is referred to as someone with "good (or, clean) character," meaning that he has not had sexual experience outside his marriage. However, a double standard is an open secret in Palashpur. A man's reputation for "bad character" is often overlooked or forgotten if he is well-off or if he has a good job. A village father, for example, was told about a young man's moral looseness in Palashpur. He replied, "Many young men have those habits. He will be all right after his marriage." At least three men in the village have raped Santal tribal women. One man was jailed for six years, and two fled from the village. Santal men caught one of the men and were about to beat him to death, but upon hearing the news, hundreds of Palashpur youth banded together and went to his rescue. One of the high-caste youths said, "Of course we don't approve of his 'bad character,' but we won't allow the Majhis [the local name for the Santal] to take the law into their hands. After all, he is a man of our village, and we must protect him."

High-caste men who indulge in premarital or extramarital affairs target primarily untouchable women. In former times (but sometimes now, too) untouchable men and women felt helpless without the patronage of high-caste *manibs,* hence the exploitation of women was easier. Some high-caste men take sexual advantage of the poverty of untouchable women. During the past five years there have been two abortions (one among the Lohar and one among the Dom) and two illegitimate births (both Lohar) resulting from these nonmarital affairs. Young Brahman men were involved in all instances. When an unmarried Lohar girl becomes pregnant, if she discloses the name of the baby's father, men of the Lohar community call for a meeting and demand a fine from the high-caste man. A wine party is given with the money and when the baby is born the girl's father adopts him. Although the girl's prospect of marriage with a bachelor is lost, she may have a *sanga,* and her child will not suffer from the social stigma.

A tragic incident occurred in Palashpur following the attempted rape of a young married Baen woman by a twenty-four-year-old Brahman bachelor. The young man was already known throughout the untouchable community for his promiscuity. His wedding was arranged and wedding date set, but one day the young woman saw him following her while she was gathering firewood from the bush. She was frightened and ran home to tell her husband, who asked her to continue collecting fuel. The Baen husband called some of his friends and quietly entered the bush just in time to find the Brahman molesting his wife. The seven Baen men jumped upon the Brahman and beat him, but high-caste men who heard the noise intervened on behalf of the Brahman. The Baen men went back to the village grudgingly and decided to file a court case. The Baen wanted several Lohar to accompany them to the police station, but the Lohar men decided against it because they and their children worked as *mahinders* in high-caste homes. They were fearful of creating possible tension with their *manibs'* families. The police from Bolpur came with a warrant to arrest the young Brahman, but he had already run away. Apparently the young man's family was ashamed of his behavior and refused to help him. This annoyed the high-caste youths, one of whom told a group of Baen men, "You should be ashamed of yourselves. We could have settled the matter like *bhadrolok,* but you went to court to act against your own people and to ruin the guy's life." But later a Baen man wondered aloud, "Who's a *bhadrolok* and who's not? It's not written on your skin. Your behavior must show it. We have suffered for many years. Those high-caste men have insulted our women on many occasions. Now we must have justice!" Another shouted, "I shall have no sleep until that guy goes to jail for at least ten years."

The search went on, but the police could not trace the young man. After three days news came that he had jumped in front of a train at Guskara Station near Bolpur and after several hours had died. Upon hearing this, high-caste men in Palashpur went into a great rage against the Baen. Some shouted, "We will burn the Muchipara" (the portion of the village where the Baen live). The Baen were frightened by this and met with CPM members at Shyambati, about a mile from Palashpur on the Palashpur-Santiniketan road. There they announced their challenge that they would fight back. Now the village was divided into two groups. When the man's body was returned, a silence fell over the community. People were ready for a storm, but one elderly Baen woman who could not bear the sight of the dead body cried loudly and ran to the home of the dead man: "Oh, he is our son, a son of the village! I saw him as a crawling baby, so big and so healthy. Oh god, why don't you take old people like us? Here we are and he is gone. How can his parents bear this?" She began to beat her chest, and soon other untouchable women, in tears, followed her.

At first the family of the dead man did not react, then abruptly the young man's mother started to cry and pound her chest. She cried loudly. After a few minutes the people set aside their grudge against each other and lamented the tragedy. The Baen men came to the Brahman's courtyard. One said, "Oh god, we did not want this. We just wanted to threaten him. After all, he was not that bad." One old Brahman man said, "What he did, all of us did in our youth. He was just very unlucky to get caught this way." During the cremation, a huge crowd gathered to lament his death, and the funeral feast was attended by both high caste and untouchables alike. The entire event was like a social drama, turning the village scoundrel into a hero. The incident also demonstrated the rising power and determination of the Baen to react against social injustices within the community.

The event also revealed the inherent community cohesiveness—to be able to stand together in the face of a calamity.

Village cohesiveness was also shown in an earlier incident of attempted armed robbery. On a new-moon night about forty people raided the house of one of the two richest Brahmans in the village. The robbers came armed with hand grenades and other weapons, and with long, lighted bamboo poles. After breaking through several doors, they made their way into the ground floor rooms of the house. Villagers heard the commotion and hundreds of men ran to the Brahman's home. Untouchable men brought bows and arrows, and whatever other weapons they had at hand. High-caste men too came with their arms. The owner of the house had a gun which he fired several times, wounding (or possibly killing) two of the thieves. The villagers surrounded the house and challenged the thieves, but the owner shouted, "Let them leave. Two of them are lying on the ground." The untouchables were about to fire their arrows when the owner again shouted, "Give them way. Let them leave. We've got two of them." So the villagers let the robbers leave, only to discover that the thieves had carried away the wounded (or dead) men.

The incident illustrates a sense of collective identity shown by the villagers. The rich owner was not a particularly popular man. Indeed, many villagers envied him and some held grudges against him, but in the face of a serious threat, villagers at all levels of the social strata banded together to protect him.

Youth Groups in Palashpur

In Palashpur there are two high-caste youth organizations, one in Pubpara and another in Paschimpara. The Pubpara organization is very active under the leadership of a Brahman college graduate. The youth organization does not have a planned agenda for their social work, but whenever the young leader visits home on vacations he becomes a catalyst for action. A group of idle young high-caste men gather around him, and they plan to do something for the village. Recently, for example, the group cut trees, and with the help of a carpenter built many benches for the local school. On another occasion they collected money to buy a bicycle for an untouchable girl's dowry. They also raised funds within the community for a family whose house had burned down. The following year they arranged a community feast for local children. They collected rice and vegetables to feed all children of the community.

Their annual event is a community Kali worship organized with contributions from Palashpur and surrounding communities. This is a recent celebration, since Palashpur already has an ancient Kali-worship place. During the festival the Baen drummers play free of charge, and untouchable men help build a huge tarpaulin tent. Rice and vegetables are donated from every home of the village. Brahman youths cook food for at least fifteen hundred people. Untouchable men, women, and children from Palashpur and surrounding communities join the feast. High-caste people also join, though they sit in separate rows.

In recent years, Paschimpara high-caste youth have also formed a youth organization. They too arrange their own celebration of Kali worship. Plays are performed by young high-caste girls up to fourteen years of age, and boys hold a swimming contest. Children of both sexes compete in recitations. Untouchable children are usually excluded from these events, but recently when the young boys' team played soccer and held a *hadudu* (a group game) tournament, two skilled untouchable boys joined the team. A considerable amount of rivalry exists between the two youth groups.

Untouchable youths of Palashpur also have informal organizations, but in this case the organizations exist for the purpose of singing *bolan* and Bhadu songs. (*Bolan* refers to the group singing of devotional songs that describe the romantic union of Lord Krishna and his consort, Radha. The songs deal with Radha's deep joys and sorrows. Bhadu is described later.) Young men, who are usually bachelors, get together in the evening to practice the songs to be performed during festivals. Baen drummer and flutists join them. High-caste men, who enjoy the *bolan* songs, encourage *bolan* groups to perform for them on festival days. For their recital, the group receives a small fee.

Bolan songs contain a gentle expression of feminized devotion for Krishna's consort. Such Vaisnava demonstration of feminine surrender is sometimes inaccurately interpreted as a homosexual trait among Hindu men (Carstairs 1957). This interpretation is a misunderstanding of sex-role ideologies in Indian society, where nurturing is not associated with mothers only. Men too take care of babies. "Feminine" traits of devotion are expected in men too, because humility and gentleness—attributes often associated with femininity—have significant spiritual power which is necessary to attain the religious path of devotional worship. Although *bolan* is performed by untouchable men only, such Vaisnava faith is an important aspect of high-caste Hindu religious philosophy. Men and women from both caste strata follow this.[11]

In addition to *bolan,* young untouchable men sing Bhadu songs throughout the month of Bhadra (between August and September). Three Bhadu groups live in Palashpur: two are from the Lohar caste and one is from the Baen caste. The groups wander through the village as well as surrounding villages, visiting each household. They carry with them a finely painted image of a young girl, which is manufactured by local Chhutor men from straw plastered with clay. Bhadu celebrations continue throughout the month and end by immersing the image in the river. Legend says that Bhadu or Bhadrabati was the name of a princess of Burdwan. She died on her wedding day at the age of fifteen. The king became so grief stricken that his subjects decided to make the princess immortal by observing this festival.

Bhadu Songs

Bhadu songs express the tender affection of fathers toward their marriageable daughters. As living folklore, the traits of Bhadu's character have changed over time. Now, a Bhadu is often described as a girl going to college on a bicycle with "side-bags."

11. In the Vaisnava school of Hindu religion—known as Bhaktibad—a devotee should identify himself with the Gopis (the milkmaids of Vridavana, the legendary abode of Lord Krishna, when Lord Krishna was a young cowherd). The Gopis were the companions of Sri Radha, Krishna's consort (the female form of the Supreme Being); they supported Radha's union with Lord Krishna. The selfless devotion of the Gopis, who themselves loved Krishna, symbolizes a spiritual devotion of the human soul for the Supreme Being. It is thus considered important for a man to surrender his masculine ego to be able to achieve the tenderness of the devotional state.

The songs express parents' anxiety about their daughters' growing up and getting married. One of the songs describes the king's daughter as follows:

Our Bhadu, the king's daughter
    is very stubborn,
Her youth is wasted,
    she is not married yet.
Bhadu walks straight
    with a proud gait.
When Bhadu was a baby,
    she was such a good girl.
I don't know why
    she has changed so much.
My Bhadu now wears a clean, crisp sari,
    and holds books in her hand.
Takes a lady's umbrella
    and goes to high school.
She smiles and talks of romances.
She stops speaking in Bengali,
    and starts in English.
Ahibhushan[12] has become insane and says,
"If I can meet Bhadu,
    I shall fulfill my desire.
By saying a few words to her,
I want to put *sindur* on her feet.
    My Bhadu is a very kind girl."

Another Bhadu song says,

Bhadu, it was not nice of you to break your parents' heart.
I don't know how she left home and never came back.
Now we watch you in Kaliyuga.[13]
You go to college with snow-powder on your face.

12. Ahibushan is the name of the poet. The song begins with fatherly affection, but the poet turns into a devotee bowing to a mother goddess, as noted by the fact that one puts *sindur* at the feet of a mother goddess.

13. Kaliyuga is one of the four time periods (*yugas*) described in Hindu mythology: (1) Satya, (2) Dwapara, (3) Treta, and (4) Kali. Kali is the present age, described as the dark age or the time of catastrophe.

Young boys make remarks at your beauty.
Oh, Bhadu, it is time for you to get married.
I, Khudiram,[14] offer *sindur* to your feet.

In thirty contemporary songs, Bhadu is referred to variously as a princess, the daughter of Madan Raj, his wife Padmabati, and as an everyday young girl. In most songs she is depicted as a local girl becoming too modern to suit her parents' standards.

The Bhadu festival begins with a short ritual worship by untouchable women, and this ritual is repeated every evening before the party starts visiting house to house. Bhadu's image is placed in the middle of a courtyard of a house, and the songs and dances are performed in front of the image. On the last day, when the young men carry Bhadu in a procession, many of them cry at the thought of parting with her. The emotional attachment becomes very deep, as the mother of a young Baen man described: "When my twenty-year-old son came home after the immersion, he started to sob, as if he had lost his own daughter. He did not eat anything that evening and was depressed for several days."

Bhadu songs are performed only by untouchable men, yet they entertain the entire community. When high-caste men and women are asked about Bhadu, the most common response is, "Bhadu is not just any particular diety. She is just like our own daughter, Gharer Laxmi [the goddess of grace and prosperity worshiped at home], who brings happiness into the household." Although the songwriters and the singers of Bhadu are untouchables, the description of Bhadu reminds one of high-caste girls commonly seen around Palashpur or Santiniketan. For example, another Bhadu song says,

Bhadu of Kaliyuga attends high school.
How beautifully she pleats her green-bordered sari!
It is ten o'clock, time for Bhadu's school.
She wears shoes and holds a lady's umbrella.
She wears her hair braided and takes a side-bag.
Young boys are after Bhadu and watch her all the time.
Khudiram says, Bhadu goes to school.
It will look so beautiful if we put *sindur* on her feet.

14. Khudiram is the name of the poet.

The picture painted in this song is fairly realistic in that several young girls from Palashpur do attend a school at Paruldanga, a semiurban area close to Santiniketan. Their school uniform is a white sari with green border, and these girls often carry a lady's umbrella (needed in both the summer and during the rainy season), and they often use cotton side-bags.

In the original legend Bhadu was a princess, remote from the day-to-day lives of untouchable men. In contemporary songs, Bhadu is a high-caste girl equally distant from the untouchables. The tender emotion and fatherly affection expressed in these songs may symbolize an idealized image of the father-daughter bond. In everyday life, one often notes a father's affection toward female children, sometimes expressed in a protective way to avoid the mother's disciplinary treatment.

Dharmaraj *Puja* Festivals

Currently, one important community organization is the Dharmaraj *puja* committee, consisting of high-caste men only. The committee oversees the celebration of the village diety, Dharmaraj, with a grand celebration for three days and nights. In earlier times only the Brahmans of the political body *dharam sarkar* controlled the activities, but now non-Brahman high-caste men join the committee. Recently, a non-Brahman Kaivarta schoolteacher was selected for the first time in the history of Palashpur to officiate as secretary of the organization. The temple fund consists of money collected from the *devatta* land and also from generous contributions from most households of the village. Dharmaraj *puja* was originally an untouchable celebration, especially of the Dom, but eventually the Brahmans became attracted by the efficacy of the *puja* and accepted the non-Brahmanic deity as their own (Mitra 1972). Dharmapuja is now an important annual event of intense intercaste communication and cooperation, with major participation by the untouchables.

A Brahman officiates as priest and performs the sacrifice of goats and sheep on the last day of the festival. Along with the Brahman, a Handi priest needs to be there to sacrifice a pig. Some say pig sacrifice was the original custom when the ceremony belonged to the untouchables. Later, when the Brahmans took over, they introduced goat and sheep sacrifice. On the second day of the festival, a phallic-shaped wooden pole representing Dharmaraj is carried to all households (except for Baen households, which are ritually polluted because of their association with cowhide) by a Lohar, Handi, or Dom ritual devotee (*bhaktya*), with a Baen drummer and a Brahman priest in attendance. One member in each household must fast until the pole arrives. After receiving offerings from all high-caste homes, the pole is taken to untouchable homes. Now the Brahman priest retires and a non-Brahman officiates in untouchable homes.

Despite apparent discrimination against them, the Baen perform an indispensable role in the festival, a role that is significant for understanding caste ideology. In 1981 there were 275 drummers who came from outside Palashpur, but committee records show that ten years earlier there had been more than six hundred drummers at the festivals. Baen guests come to offer their performances free of charge as a dedication to the deity. (Under normal circumstances Baen drummers receive forty rupees a day for their performances.) The committee assigns individual high-caste households to host Baen drummers and feed them three times a day. The committee also offers one kilogram of wine to each drummer (distributed at the liquor store by the Sundi), and money for their transportation.

Baen drummers have a special ceremony called "the roar of thunder." The drummers, old and young—and some children who carry smaller drums—stand in a circle playing their drums with skill and exuberant energy. This ceremony honors Lord of the Clouds, one of the emissaries of Dharmaraj. Crowds of men, women, and children gather excitedly to watch the performance. After the ceremony the drummers play and dance in a procession through the village. The crowd follows them, and children run freely back and forth cheering the drummers.

In 1982 the number of drummers decreased suddenly to 107. Apparently the Baen had become sensitive about the negligence of the high-caste families, who were feeding them inferior food. The *upa-pradhan* (the Baen village chief) in Palashpur told his fellowmen, "When you go as their guests, they serve you in the corner of the courtyard as if you were dogs. You must not go to their homes." Another Baen woman said, "Our men carry huge drums on their backs. These are over forty or fifty pounds. They dance for hours carrying these drums on their backs. After such work, if you serve them just rice and vegetables [meaning no fish, meat, or dessert], you cannot expect them to come again." The Dharmaraj *puja* committee in Palashpur became concerned after that year's experience. Committeemen are now considering ways to please the Baen drummers so they will continue to come to Palashpur as they have in the past. The experience of the committee indicates again a rising consciousness about injustices in intercaste social relations. However, several Brahmans in the village were taken aback by the reaction of the Baen. They could not understand why the Baen should be offended at not being treated as equals. Many high-caste people, however, recognize that their social relationships with "inferior castes" need to be modified and perhaps reexamined.

Dharmaraj *puja* is truly a festival of the entire community. After the three-day ritual ends, it is followed by days of entertainment, with all-night traditional and modern plays performed by professional companies on an open stage, puppet shows, many sessions of *bolan* songs, and a fair. Men, women and children from Palashpur and nearby villages gather by the hundreds. Themes from these plays confirm the Brahmanical ethos of husband-wife and mother-son relationships. Powerful mothers but passive wives are often shown as ideal. Mature, dominant, but affectionate women are idealized mother images. In fact women are sometimes deified in their roles as mothers and as chaste women. "Modern" women wearing Western slacks and carrying cigarettes, on the other hand, are often depicted as evil characters who sometimes repent after suffering and surrender to their men as submissive wives. Spectators boo undesirable characters such as these "liberated" women, and they applaud the chaste, submissive wives.

Children of all castes stay awake throughout the night during these performances, sitting in the front rows on the three sides of the stage. Children are never separated from adult company on any of the festival occasions. During Dharmapuja children of all ages move among the adults, running around and playing games. If they are unruly, an adult—perhaps a parent or a village uncle—may scold them or even slap them, but they are never excluded from the center of excitement. Children expect to wear new clothing during the festival (young *mahinders* receive their annual clothing at this time, for example), but many poor children are disappointed when they receive nothing. The community festival thus shows how a villager's social universe is determined by his caste group. Caste rules are relaxed during the period of intense intercaste cooperation, but ultimately the festival serves to reinforce caste distinctions.

CHAPTER 4

Growing up in Palashpur

The Family and the Individual

High-caste Hindus in Palashpur often live in extended families, with three generations (grandparents and their married sons, sons' wives, and children, as well as unmarried sons and unmarried daughters) sharing a common cooking hearth. In extended families such as these, married brothers and their families share the same hearth after their parents die. The eldest brother acts as head of the household, and his wife oversees food preparation and other daily necessities of the entire family. Some high-caste Hindus who have moved to Palashpur from outside the village live in nuclear families, with just the husband, wife, and children forming the domestic unit. A few untouchables live in extended families, but unlike high-caste families, most untouchables live in nuclear families. Newlyweds at all caste levels tend to live close to the groom's parents, and after one or two years of marriage they usually create their own kitchen if they do not already have one.

Brahman households vary in size, from three people in a nuclear family to twenty in an extended family. Among non-Brahman high-caste families, households vary in size from two to six people. Two untouchable families, however, have ten members each.[1]

Some Indianists argue that hierarchical relationships within an extended or joint family are dependent primarily on sex but also on age (see Kakar 1979; Inden and Nicholas 1977). Despite the structural superiority of males, however, hierarchical superordination of a person in Palashpur is not always determined by gender. Indeed, there is an asymmetry of status between husband and wife, but the personality of a family member (see also Roland 1982)—especially a woman—can give her an authoritative role as a mother, wife, grandmother, or even as a sister-in-law. The norm of male superiority is often inapplicable in everyday social relationships within high-caste families.

Child socialization in Palashpur, as documented at length in chapter 7, is influenced by caste and sex role. Caste identification develops early in childhood, but sex-role identification does not become clear until about age five. By this time children are socialized not only to accept their social positions as caste members, but also to accept the caste ideology of their roles as males and females. Below and especially in chapter 7 we show how children from the two main caste strata grow up in different social universes, experiencing different forms of parental care and role models.

Children in High-Caste Families

High-caste children grow up with a variety of adults looking after them.[2] Mothers, however, are usually the primary caretakers of children, though grandmothers may assume this re-

1. Villagers with sufficient land usually prefer to live in extended families, with land serving as the basis for common property. Among the untouchables, both of the families with many members are *bhagchasis* over more than twenty *bighas* of land.

2. Even in nuclear families, neighbors play an important role in child care, thereby creating for the child bonds with other adults, almost as if they were members of an extended or joint family.

sponsibility if the mother gives birth while the child is still young. While keeping an eye on their children, women of high-caste families engage in domestic labor such as preparing puffed rice, and boiling and drying paddy—in addition to their regular chores of cooking meals and washing. Young girls and often boys also take care of babies, and two-year-olds may move from one lap to another among members of the joint family or among neighbors. Very young children are sometimes the center of attraction in a group of people, be it in a tea shop or at home. Young children are never excluded from adult company, and they are not allowed to cry for long. Male and female babies are dressed alike. Both wear bright colors, homemade eye makeup which is believed to be good for the eyes, and jingling bells on their feet.

Babies are weaned casually unless the mother is pregnant with another child. A grandmother is likely to "suckle" the older baby on her wizened breasts. Toilet training, too, is fairly casual. To toilet the baby, mothers and grandmothers let the young sit between their outstretched legs close to their ankles. Young babies and children share their mother's bed until they are eight or nine years old. Sometimes daughters sleep with their mothers for a much longer period, and sons sleep in a separate room with their fathers. Young children of both sexes are allowed to stay naked much of the time, especially around bathing time.

An important part of daily child care of older infants and toddlers is assumed by older siblings, especially sisters. Eight-year-old Pali Saha's mother, for example, has four children. Pali's mother is often too busy with her work to bathe her infant daughter and to massage the baby with mustard oil.[3] So Pali and her sixty-year-old grandmother assume these tasks. Pali goes to the field each day to defecate and takes along her five-year-old sister, Mili, and her three-year-old brother. After that they wash themselves in the pond under Pali's supervision. Pali is also re-

3. Housekeeping in rural India is a time-consuming activity. Women fetch water from an outside tap, wash clothes at a community pond, and collect firewood for cooking. They prepare two hot meals a day (unless they are too poor, as are many of the untouchables). Domestic chores are performed without benefit of electricity or gas. Women in most high-caste homes boil and dry paddy, and prepare puffed rice in huge quantities for daily breakfasts and snacks.

sponsible for cleaning her brother and eight-month-old baby sister if they urinate or defecate during the day. Babies are not dressed in diapers, and are washed immediately after they wet themeselves or have a bowel movement. Pali keeps an eye on the young children all day except when she is in school. She often carries her baby sister on her hip and holds the hand of her brother. She visits the home of her Lohar neighbor whom she addresses as her "aunty" (*kakima*, or more specifically, father's younger brother's wife, used here in a fictive sense). After reaching the Lohar house, Pali places her baby sister on the lap of the old grandfather of her Lohar friend. (Pali addresses him as *dadu*, meaning "grandpa.")

Since Pali's younger sister, Mili, was born, Pali has shared her grandmother's bed at night. Pali is also very close to her grandmother, who is protective of Pali and does not allow her mother to discipline her. Pali's father works long hours at Visva Bharati University. He gets angry if Pali neglects her schoolwork, as she sometimes does; as a result he has arranged for a tutor to coach her for about one-and-one-half hours every evening. Pali's grandmother, a devout Hindu widow who believes strongly in caste distinctions, has trained Pali not only to be responsible for her brother and sister but also to observe specific caste rules. Before leaving home to play with a Lohar friend, for example, Pali takes off her own clothes and the clothes of her baby brother and sister. The children wear only their underwear, thus avoiding the need to have to wash their clothes after visiting an untouchable neighbor. Pali and Mili take *doob* in the pond and then simply change into clean, "unpolluted" underwear. (*Doob* refers to immersing oneself in a pond to ritually cleanse oneself after coming into polluting physical contact with an untouchable.)

The three-year-old son of the Lohar neighbor sometimes goes to Pali's house to play. He has already learned that he is allowed only in Pali's courtyard, but not on the porch. Pali's grandmother and mother make sure that the child does not touch any washed clothes hanging on the line, nor does he touch any water pots. Once a group of high-caste girls played in front of Pali's house. Two Baen girls came to join them, and Pali yelled, "Don't take them in. I have to wash my clothes then." Ignoring her plea, her friends began playing with the Baen girls, and Pali left the game.

These Brahman children bathe and wash their clothes in the pond every day after playing, hence they feel free to play with untouchable children. However only in Paschimpara, where there are several Brahman homes adjacent to untouchable homes, are such intercaste peer relationships tolerated. Nonetheless, after taking their daily *doob,* Brahman girls are not allowed to come close to their untouchable friends again.[4] Children do not appear to hold these intercaste regulations against each other. In fact, the Lohar and Pali's Sundi-caste families are very close. They rely on each other and help each other in need. Still the caste distinction is constantly recognized and asserts the hierarchical superiority of the Sundi over the Lohar. The Lohar neighbors appear to accept this without bitterness. Even though the caste system segregates people, it also helps keep the sociocultural system integrated by keeping each caste in its own place within a network of known interdependencies.

Pali's grandmother initiated Pali into observing an "evening worship" ritual (*sanjpujani brata*) that should be continued each day for four consecutive years. This ritual is meant for young girls so that they may eventually acquire good homes, husbands, and children. Pali and six of her high-caste (Brahman and Bene) girlfriends perform the ritual with great care. The chantings in simple Bengali ask for a good home, children, gold jewelry, a faithful husband, good harvests, many kitchen tools, a rice pounder, prosperity for in-laws, parents, and maternal relatives, and particularly for no co-wives.[5]

4. On one occasion during a Bhadu performance—with singing, dancing, and drumming—a small group of Brahman girls could not resist coming to Muchipara after they had already taken their *doob.* They stood together, reminding their Baen friends that they must not touch them because they were wearing *kacha* clothes. When teased by the field anthropologist who said, "I have *akacha* clothes. I am going to touch you," the girls ran away, giggling. (*Akacha* means clothes that have come in contact with other people, especially untouchables; and *kacha* means washed clothes that have not been in contact with untouchables.)

5. Co-wives are associated with the traditional practice of polygyny among the Kulin Brahmans, a custom that is no longer in vogue. Previously, a Kulin Brahman girl could marry only another Kulin Brahman. But since keeping one's daughter unmarried was considered a great sin, Kulin Brahman men often married many wives without supporting them. These wives passed their lives in their parents' homes. During the second half of the nineteenth century, social

Pali's mother can sometimes be very harsh with her. One afternoon after school, for example, Pali was ready to have her snack but first she was supposed to arrange clothes on the line. The line came off the hook and she yelled, "Ma, come see what happened!" Pali's mother, who was having her own midday meal, got up and slapped Pali severely. Pali's father, who was home that day, shouted "Why are you beating her for nothing?" Pali's mother left the courtyard angrily. She had been in a bad mood since her argument with her mother-in-law (Pali's grandmother) in the morning. Later a neighbor said, "She beats her children whenever she is angry with her husband or mother-in-law."

Pali's mother has given birth to three daughters and only one son. This has caused great distress in the family. Her grandmother said bitterly in the presence of her grandchildren, "Look at these girls. They will have to be married off with cash dowry. I choke when I think about it. I just hope they will be happily married." High-caste girls in Palashpur grow up with such constant reminders of being a liability to the family, especially if there is more than one daughter in the family. Nonetheless, girls are usually treated with compassion because they are destined eventually to go to "a stranger's home." Many fathers address their daughters as "ma," little mother, expressing an affectionate bond between the two of them.[6] Fathers rarely punish girls physically or even use harsh words toward them, though such behavior is expected from mothers, who are responsible for their daughters reputations as "good girls" or "bad girls." In this regard, a Bengali proverb says, the quality of clarified butterfat (*ghee*) depends on the quality of the cow; so does the quality of the daughter depend on the mother.

---

reformers attacked this social injustice and eventually succeeded in abolishing the custom. A postindependence law also prohibits any Hindu from accepting a second wife. The system of polygyny disappeared long ago from Palashpur. Indeed, as early as 1933, only one Brahman home contained two wives (Ali 1960).

6. Kakar (1979) cites several examples from Vedic rites to show how much the daughters were neglected in the family rituals of traditional India. Such neglect is apparent in the patriarchal rites of a family. However, a well-known Sanskrit proverb also says, One who brings joy and happiness into the family, she is called the joyful (daughter). This proverb signifies the affectionate bond between daughters and their parents. Even though they do not fulfill the same instrumental needs as sons, daughters fulfill important emotional needs.

The birth of a boy is celebrated with greater joy than the birth of a girl, but overall baby girls in Palashpur are not discriminated against. Both baby boys and girls enjoy warmth and physical contact with the men and women of the family and neighborhood.[7] Both high-caste and untouchable fathers carry babies, as do young boys. Even a Brahman boy of eleven who is considered by the villagers to be a brat carried his three-year-old sister on the front seat of his bicycle. The boy did not have an older sister and his mother had a small baby, so he was required to take care of his baby sister after school hours. When he played soccer his sister sat in one corner of the playground. Occasionally she whimpered and he ran to console her, then returned to his game. A Napit boy of eleven spent most of his time in a Brahman neighbor's home during the summer vacation babysitting for the Brahman's two-year-old granddaughter. The boy performed this service for free because families in Palashpur have no custom of paying for babysitting. Such child care is usually done by elder sisters or brothers, but if no sibling or grandparent is available, a neighbor's child babysits.

Children of both sexes play together and are indulged until the age of five or six. When boys become too rough, however, mothers may yell, "You are a boy. Why don't you go play with other boys!" Nonetheless, many boys between the ages of six and nine continue to play with girls if no other boys are available. The transition to sex-segregated groupings seems to be gradual, though boys from the age of nine or ten seldom play with girls, and they seldom play close to home.[8] Rather they roam the village, playing games quite far from home. In this way,

7. Miller (1978) associates the higher mortality rate among baby girls than boys in northwestern India with neglect of female babies. This negligence seems to result from the burden of having to provide dowry at marriage and from the subsequent loss of these girls' economic contribution to the family. Death-rate figures for girls versus boys in Palashpur (ages one month through six years in both caste strata) during the past fifteen years fail to reveal the same trend in higher female infant mortality. The issue of gender differences in parents' treatment of children is developed at greater length in chap. 7.

8. Kakar described sudden changes in a boy's social world in northern India as an abrupt shift of socializing agents—from maternal care in a feminine world to paternal authority in a formal, masculine world. "It is the son," he wrote, "who experiences the shock . . . of maternal separation and entry into the man's world" (1979, 127). No such dramatic shift occurs in Palashpur where boys experi-

young boys adapt themselves to a wider social sphere than their sisters, who stay close to the domestic site. Occasional exceptions occur, though. One nine-year-old boy in Pubpara, for example, played with girls most of the time. He disliked the roughness of the boy's games, but seemed quite comfortable with the girls—and his mother did not worry about his playing with girls.

Young high-caste girls play games either in their courtyards or on the road in front of their houses. They sometimes wear just their underpants, but when they get a bit older they cover their bare chests with dresses, and they quit "playing house"; they then engage in other games such as jump rope and hopscotch. Girls must also learn to perform household chores, including cleaning the courtyard, fetching water, and washing dishes. And it is a girl's duty to light the evening lamp and to blow a conch shell three times in the evening. This is an auspicious ritual to be performed by girls or young wives to "bring blessings and prosperity into the home." Every home has a holy basil-plant with a mound as an altar. An oil lamp is lighted at the altar, where members of the family bow their heads in a moment of prayer.

High-caste girls in Palashpur are often absent from school because, as they say, "My brother did not feel well," or "I did the cooking today because my mother is not well" (meaning she is menstruating), or "I had some extra housework to do." Most girls stop attending school at the age of thirteen or fourteen, by which time some have reached Class VIII (the eighth grade) at the local school. Very few continue further study outside the village.

The majority of high-caste boys also drop out of school after completing Class VIII, though in recent years some have gone on for higher education. Many of the younger children are tutored after school by young unemployed high-caste men in the village who are hired for this purpose. A common scene in the village is to find three or four boys studying in a group with their tutor.

---

ence less presssure to conform to their male role. The nurturing role of caretaking is also interchangeable between the sexes in Palashpur.

When they are not studying their lessons after school, boys from the age of ten onward congregate at the school playground or in a large playground on the western outskirts of the village. There they play soccer, hockey, or cricket, with simple homemade equipment. On other occasions, three or four boys together climb trees or collect sugarcane from the field. High-caste boys often include untouchable boys—their schoolmates—in their games, though the number of untouchables is small because most of them need to work after school. Some high-caste boys imitate untouchable boys by riding a buffalo with Lohar cowherds in a game called *moshchora*. This game is disapproved of by high-caste parents, who scold the boys if they catch them with the cowherds. Mothers complain about their boys being very careless about caste rules and about the boys wandering so far from home, but mothers recognize they cannot keep a continuous eye on their boys.

Boys are usually more pampered by women in the family than are girls, and boys are given preference in food distribution. This sex distinction becomes especially conspicuous as the boys get older. The preferential treatment of boys is most evident in families with siblings of both sexes above the age of nine or ten. For example, in a Satgop family of two girls and one boy, an uncle who had caught two medium-sized fish exclaimed, "We four will share these two fish, one-half to each of us." The ten-year-old girl said matter-of-factly—without any apparent resentment or disappointment—"No, Grandma will serve the fish only to the boys, you and elder brother." High-caste men and boys are served first at a family dinner, and they are served the best of every dish, especially milk, fish, and eggs. Girls are told, "The boys need more for their health. A sister should be affectionate to her brothers and feed them well."

By the age of eight—when the girls are asked to perform domestic chores—they begin to recognize some of the disadvantages of their gender. Boys too begin to recognize themselves as the preferred ones (see chap. 7 for an elaboration of this point), and they enjoy the freedom of being able to move about the village and pastures. But girls experience restrictions all about them. They are expected to stay close to their mothers and other women of the neighborhood, and in this way they learn much about the proper behavior of women. High-caste boys, on the other hand, spend more time with peers and have less exposure to adult company. Nonetheless, young boys are often found in the company of elder brothers, cousins, and uncles.

As boys and girls grow older, they have less and less physical contact with their mothers and other adults. Moreover, in the Bengali sociocultural system children only occasionally experience direct and overt expressions of affection. Kissing on the head or touching the chin of a child and then kissing the child's hand are the most typical expressions of physical affection. Older children of nine onward may be patted on their back or caressed gently on their head and face, but the most common forms of approval are expressed nonverbally by the parent with a glance or a smile. Direct verbal praise to the children is reported to be minimal, though as shown below, it does occur. Mothers generally prefer to praise the child to others when the child is absent. It is also considered poor taste to praise one's own child too much; it is like "praising oneself." Mothers may, however, tell their husbands or other children about the child's qualities, or they may point to the child as an example for younger children to emulate—and the recipient of these compliments may overhear the remarks. Grandparents and other older members of the family, on the other hand, may praise or criticize a child more directly.

The widespread cultural ideology in India that disapproves of direct praise of children by parents seems often to be informally disregarded in Palashpur—at least in private—because well over 90 percent of the sample children described in chapter 7 responded affirmatively on the Parental Acceptance-Rejection Questionnaire (described in chap. 6) to questions about being praised by their mothers. Moreover, all (100 percent) of the mothers of these children responded in the same way when they reflected on their own childhood experiences.[9]

9. To be more specific, four items on the Parental Acceptance-Rejection Questionnaire (PARQ), noted in the following table, inquire about being praised by one's mother. For example, one of the items says, "My mother praises me when I deserve it." Adults and children respond to items such as this by checking one of four response options: "almost always true," "sometimes true," "rarely true," and "almost never true." The table below shows that 55 percent or more of both

As the boys grow older, the primary responsiblity of disciplining them shifts gradually from the women to fathers or other adult males. Fathers, however, are not strict or authoritarian. On the contrary, adult men appear to be quite nurturing, both with high-caste and untouchable children. Nonetheless, women, because of their central role within the family, tend to exercise more direct influence in a child's socialization. This is especially true because most high-caste men spend long hours each day with other men, at the tea shops or elsewhere.

The usual way of admonishing a child about his misdeeds is to say, "Others will talk about you or call you a bad boy (or bad girl)," or "Don't bring shame on us," or, when trying to correct a child's habits, "Try to be like Sanjit. Don't you see how every-

---

children and adults in the sample responded "almost always true" to all the items; 94 percent or more of the respondents answered "sometimes true" or "almost always true" to all but one of the items (which was answered by 88 percent of the children.)

Percentage of Children and Mothers Who Reported Being Praised by Their Parents

	PARQ RESPONSE OPTION		
	Sometimes True	Almost Always True	Total Affirmative[a]
Child PARQ			
My mother:			
1 says nice things about me	31%	63%	94%
19 praises me to others	33	55	88
26 praises me when I deserve it	16	80	96
36 tells how proud she is of me	35	61	96
Adult PARQ			
My mother:			
1 said nice things about me	14	86	100
19 praised me to other	26	74	100
26 praised me when I deserved it	24	74	98
36 told how proud she was of me	38	60	98

a. The difference between the "total affirmative" reported and 100 percent reveals the percentage that answered "rarely true" or "never true" to items inquiring about being praised in childhood.

one praises him?" There is no Bengali expression comparable to "I am proud of you." Parents' usual expression of pride or approval is a smile or pat on the back or perhaps an approving nod. Parents do not usually tease children, but older siblings and cousins sometimes tease each other a lot. Children sometimes respond to teasing by yelling back or complaining to their mothers. A mother is expected to be protective of her children. In fact, a mother will be criticized most if she is either nonprotective or not disciplinarian enough. Throughout the untouchable portion of the community in particular, villagers refer to a woman as a "good mother" or as a "harsh mother." A protective mother is a "good mother." There is of course considerable variation in parenting within Palashpur high-caste families. The following five short sketches show common variations in parental warmth and control.

SKETCH 1. Sabita, a ten-year-old Tambuli girl, returned from school around half-past three. Her mother served her puffed rice but Sabita complained, "I won't eat puffed rice. I want rice." Her mother retorted with irritation, "No, if you take rice you will get sick." Sabita started to cry and her mother continued sharply, "Eat what I have given you, otherwise don't eat."

SKETCH 2. Eight-year-old Bakul asked for food when she came home from school along with her elder sister and younger brother. Her mother was doing housework and said, "Wait for a while." The two sisters waited until their mother served them rice and then they went to the pond to wash their plates. They were now ready to play, but their mother said, "No game for you now. You better clean the yard, then fetch drinking water from the tap, and after that clean the kitchen. When you've finished all those things you may go out of the house."

SKETCH 3. One drizzly afternoon, eleven-year-old Urmila carried her two-year-old brother while playing with her friends in front of the house. She complained, "I can't play carrying him" and dropped him to the ground. The boy started to cry loudly and Urmila's father came out yelling, "How could you be so irresponsible? Such a big sister neglecting her baby brother!" Urmila's mother came out, took the two-year-old on her hip, and said to Urmila, "Go play now. But don't be late."

SKETCH 4. Two sisters and a younger brother were playing at home. When they started fighting, the younger brother (a six-year-old) slapped Mridula, his eight-year-old sister. Mridula started to cry, and when their mother heard it she scolded the girls, "You are such big girls. You should be ashamed of yourselves! You don't know how to behave!" She did not say a word to her son.

SKETCH 5. Raka, a six-year-old, fought with her friend who had come to play in Raka's house. The girls became nasty to each other, and Raka's mother said to the visitor, "Why don't you go home and take a bath?" After the girl left, Raka started to cry, and her mother said, "It is time for your bath, too. Let me put oil on your hair. You bathe with your sister." Raka continued to cry and her mother said, "You can go to your friend's house after your nap in the afternoon."

Some mothers are demanding of their ten- and eleven-year-old daughters and scold them if they neglect their household chores. Boys, on the other hand, are expected to do their school lessons, and they are scolded if they neglect them. However, if a boy becomes too wild his mother may threaten him, "I am going to tell your father" (or some other senior male relative), thereby shifting responsibility of discipline to a male. The most common verbal threat used against high-caste children is, "There will be no food for you"—a threat that in reality almost never materializes, but these words symbolize the withdrawal of love. Being "locked inside the house" is another common form of punishment for both boys and girls. ("Being locked inside the house" means the child is not allowed to go out of the house to play with friends.) When verbal reprimands do not work (or if the mother is irritated for some other reason), parents slap or thrash their children. On only two occasions, however, did we find high-caste fathers beating their sons severely, with canes. One boy (a ten-year-old) made faces at an outsider, and the other (a thirteen-year-old boy) did badly in school because he neglected his studies. Both of these boys are known for their continual misbehavior in the neighborhood. In most cases, the child's grandparents, senior family members, or even neighbors interfere if physical punishment becomes too harsh, though people do not decry a little slapping or hitting of children. Indeed, grown-ups often talk with pride about being slapped by their parents. This is taken as a mark of having been "properly" disciplined. However, excessive beating or depriving children of food is deplored.

Children in Palashpur address men and women of all castes in fictive kin terms according to the generation to which they belong. Father's friends of his age are called *kaka,* meaning "uncle"; father's elder brothers and their (elder) friends are called *jyatha,* meaning, in effect, "elder uncle." Similarly, daughters of Palashpur belonging to the parental generation are called "father's sister" (*pishima*). Each of these terms of address indicates not only the generation to which an individual belongs but also the individual's position in birth order. For example, *baro jyatha* means eldest uncle, and *mejo kaka* refers to the middle uncle born after one's own father. Aunts are also called by terms according to their position in generational and birth order hierarchies.

Children may address all elder cousins as "elder brother" (*dada*) or "elder sister" (*didi*), but they must also learn the kinship term for each cousin's actual relationship to them. Cousins on the father's side of the family are called by different kinship terms from cousins on the mother's side. For example, the term *jathtuto* refers to children of the father's elder brother. *Khurtuto* refers to children of the father's younger brother, and *pishtuto* refers to children of the father's sister. Cousins on the mother's side of the family are called by an equivalent set of terms. Similarly, a child addresses neighbors of his own community according to the terminology related to his father's family. When the child visits his maternal relatives and their neighbors, he addresses them according to the terminology meant for the maternal relatives. Kinship terminology is quite extensive, with separate terms for maternal uncle (*mama*), maternal aunt (*mashima*), and maternal grandparents (*dadamashai* or *dadu,* and *didima* or *dida*). Paternal grandparents are addressed differently (e.g., *thakurdada* or *dadu,* and *thakurma* or *dida*). Different terms of address are used for affinal aunts and uncles, that is, aunts and uncles who are spouses of one's consanguineous aunts and uncles.

Female Adolescence and Adulthood in High-Caste Families

By age thirteen, the polarity of sexes becomes obvious among boys and girls. Although having more restricted movement than boys, preadolescent girls visit friends in different parts of the village, and they meet their fathers, uncles, and other men at tea shops, where they are sometimes treated to sweets. These girls also watch boys' games at the playground, and they have other contacts with age-mate boys. After menarche, girls continue wearing Western-style dresses, but their movement outside the home becomes restricted. They also learn to follow strict menstruation taboos such as not touching cooking pots or water vessels. When their breasts develop visibly, girls are also expected to give up their Western style dresses, which are meant for young girls. Young women of this age should begin wearing saris, which cover their breasts and legs. But in Palashpur, many girls wear Western dresses until they become so developed physically it becomes unseemly for them to continue.

Mothers are unenthusiastic about their daughters growing up because the time for their marriage arrangements then becomes imminent. Adolescent girls stop disclosing their ages, especially to outsiders, and by this time the majority of adolescent girls stop going to school. There are seventy marriageable high-caste girls in Palashpur, out of whom only twenty-five are enrolled in school. These young women range in age from fifteen to eighteen years. Only one Brahman girl and one Satgop girl go to college. When asked about girls' education, parents most commonly answer, "What's the use of giving education to a girl? If she is more educated, you have to look for an educated groom, which costs more money."

Anxiety about educated daughters costing more money in dowry is confirmed by the experience of a Satgop family with two daughters who were college graduates. Neither daughter could find a job so they earned money by private tutoring. The father looked desperately for a groom and finally found a suitable young man with a B.A. degree. The bride's family paid ten thousand rupees cash, plus gold and other gifts in dowry. The entire dowry expense came to about twenty-five thousand rupees. Young girls in their early teens discussed this event at length and said, "See, it is not worth spending money on education. Our parents have to offer dowry anyway." In another case, a nineteen-year-old girl gave up her studies in the final year of high school because her mother became sick. The daughter had to stay home to cook, because as the mother said, "Our men are not supposed to do the cooking. After all, she has to be married as soon as possible. Why should we bother to give her more schooling?"

Young adolescent girls in Palashpur spend most of their time doing domestic chores, but sometimes they group together to sew, to read novels, or to gossip. They stop playing outdoor games altogether, but they play cards or *ludo* (a board game like Parcheesi) at home. Whereas little girls participate in creative activities such as acting, dancing, or recitations during school or village functions, older girls do not participate in any of these.

Young women of the village become excited when marriage negotiations begin for one of their cohort, and when the prospective groom and his friends come to "look at" the girl. The girls talk openly about the groom's behavior, appearance, and the dowry demand. When one of the girls does get married, the unmarrieds are eager to learn all they can about her experiences in her in-law's home. The girls also learn a great deal about sex from their married friends. But gradually, a distance grows between them and the newly married girls as the latter settle into their new lives with their in-laws.

Occasionally unmarried high-caste girls visit Bolpur to watch a movie, with an older woman as chaperone. These young women read movie magazines when they can get them, and they spend a lot of time talking about movie stars, all of which provides relief from their monotonous life as they wait—sometimes ten or fifteen years—to be married. Seventeen unmarried high-caste women from eighteen to thirty-five years of age in the village reported their lives to be drab while they waited to be married. Four of them were hostile to their families for keeping them "sitting at home." One said, "If I was allowed to attend school, I could have finished a master's degree by this time." Another said, "When you wait and wait, you cannot blame the girl if her mind goes in wrong directions."

By the age of twenty, most unmarried high-caste girls start looking pale and unhealthy. Some of them in their late twenties look old, with hollow cheeks and deepset eyes, without much of the liveliness of youth. In addition to these signs of apparent malnutrition, there is little in the life-style of these unmarried women to enhance a healthy appearance. One nineteen-year-old girl, however, had not lost her romanticism about marriage. When asked her feelings about getting married she became shy, but wrote her thoughts as follows:

> From the first day of your youth, you think about the moment of meeting your husband. How are you going to look at each other? How are you going to touch each other? All these things come into the mind of the couple. Thinking of it, the girl's heart fills with the joy of expectation. . . . She must not give him everything on the first night during *phoolsajya* (the bed decorated with flowers in the bridal chamber). If she does, he might misunderstand her as not being a "pure girl." After all, the union between a man and a woman is not just a physical union, it is a union of souls. The bridal night is just the beginning. The man must not get all he wants on the very first night.

This young woman was married some months after writing this. Her father had to sell some of his land to acquire her dowry.

Male Adolescence and Adulthood in High-Caste Families

By the age of eleven or twelve a Brahman boy must go through the sacred thread ceremony called *paita* or *upanayana*. It is important for Brahman boys to be recognized as "twice-born" (*dwija*). The sacred thread ritual signifies the rebirth of a Brahman male. It is also believed that a Brahman boy may appropriately associate with high-caste non-Brahmans until his *upanayana*. After going through this ritual, however, he should avoid physical contact with non-Brahmans. For the Brahman youth the rite is not simply an initiation into manhood; it recognizes his social position as the highest status possible in the sociocultural system. Brahman women do not have such rites, and according to the scriptured rules they whould be reckoned along with non-Brahman Sudras.

Upanayana is a long rite, involving the boy being secluded from his mother, having his head shaved, living as an ascetic, taking alms like a monk, and eventually being presented publicly into the community. Following this puberty rite, which is performed by a family priest, the youth receives gifts, money, and clothing from relatives and neighbors. He receives his sacred thread and is initiated with a sacred Vedic prayer. A large community feast is arranged for the occasion. From a very young age, high-caste boys are pampered by the womenfolk. *Upanayana* now confirms this superior status as a full Brahman male. No comparable rite exists for other high-caste boys.

Most young high-caste men in Palashpur appear healthy, in contrast to many of the young high-caste women. (Chap. 7 describes gender-based inequalities in the distribution of food, inequalities that may account for some sex differences in physical appearance.) Adolescent boys continue playing group games, but as they grow older many simply wander indolently around the village. The majority of these young men drop out of school after completing Class VIII, but even those with more education, with a few exceptions, rarely find salaried jobs. The young men typically receive pocket money from their parents, and a few are known to have temper tantrums when they do not get what they want. Some of these youths earn a little by tutoring local children; only a few are engaged in business, including four who run tea stalls, two who run rice mills, and one who runs a sweet shop.

It is a common sight in Palashpur to see young high-caste men in groups sitting idly at the tea shops, listening to transistor radios. Sometimes they congregate in small groups in the woods near the Kopai River to have a picnic, and some of the men have liquor parties without their parents' knowledge. When a twenty-two-year-old college graduate was asked, "Don't you feel bored with such an idle life?" he answered, "Not always. We travel a lot, attend political meetings, attend several village fairs in surrounding areas, and enjoy movies and smoking." The young men also talk a lot about personal romances and amorous adventures, which often seem like male fantasies in a context where women are sexually unapproachable. As noted earlier, however, some of the youths do have romantic relationships with local girls, and a few have secret sexual experiences with untouchable women. Such illicit affairs are deplored and are becoming risky because of the rising consciousness of rights within the untouchable sector of the community.

After a high-caste man reaches the age of twenty-two to twenty-five his family begins to negotiate his marriage, and his hopes for a promising fortune grow. For many, marriage with its attendant dowry is the only hope they have to make a start in life. So, these young men talk a great deal about the amount of dowry they expect to receive. Some also hope to get a job with the help of their wives' fathers or to start a new business with the cash dowry, but very few make use of the money in a profitable way. Most of the dowry is spent in feasting and merrymaking.

One handsome twenty-six-year-old son of a widow had no financial resources of his own, but he had completed schooling through Class VII. During the district election he was employed for two weeks as a temporary policeman. His boss liked him and wanted him to marry his daughter, a high school graduate. The father offered a dowry of eight *bighas* of land and gold jewelry, valued at ten thousand rupees. Such a magnificent dowry generated a great deal of talk about the young man's good fortune. During this talk the observation was made that "his father-in-law will soon have him settled down. He might even find him a job." In Palashpur, the larger the dowry, the more enhanced the man's worth is seen to be. Conversely, the smaller the dowry, the more diminished the man's worth.

Childhood and Adolescence in Untouchable Families

The economic world of Palashpur provides untouchable children with very different social experiences from those of high-caste children. These socioeconomic differences both reflect and create different caste and sex-role ideologies (see also Seymour 1975; Ullrich 1977). Rearing babies is similar among untouchable and high-caste families, although babies and toddlers in untouchable families spend more time with or near their mothers than with others. Mothers sometimes take their babies with them to work, and they sometimes leave an infant on the lap of a nearby four-year-old sibling while they finish their work. Infants and toddlers are also sometimes left under shade trees while mothers work in the field, and women regularly take their young children to work with them in high-caste homes. Being in such homes every day, young untouchable children learn very early to be careful (and fearful) around "superior people." As one Baen man put it:

> I remember visiting a Brahman home when mother worked in it. There were several children. Some of them used to play with me. I felt very happy, but the women used to yell at me for coming near the kitchen. They used to refer to me as "that son of a Baen." As I grew older [around nine or ten] some of my Brahman friends visited our home. My mother always gave them a wooden seat or some mats to sit on, and she gave them fruit. But when I went to their house, their mothers treated me like a stray dog. I gradually stopped playing with them and visiting their homes. I felt more comfortable with untouchable children.

A Lohar woman had a similar experience: "I used to accompany my aunt [the girl's mother was dead] to work in high-caste homes. Aunt was very cautious about my presence and warned me all the time, 'Don't touch that,' 'Don't go on the porch.' I was offered puffed rice and ate it sitting in a corner of the courtyard while high-caste children crowded on the porch. Gradually, I became very fearful of the high castes. Later when I went to school, I made friends with high-caste girls. These girls used to visit each others' houses, but never came to our house. I dared not visit them."

When mothers are unable to tend their offspring, untouchable toddlers and babies are often cared for by elder siblings if the siblings are not fully occupied by their own work. Untouchable mothers also sometimes leave their babies with older children or with their grandparents. By the age of five or so, however, untouchable children must learn to care for themselves because most of the women are too busy to care for them. Elder siblings too must work. Little six-year-old Chinta (a Baen girl), for example, has already become used to taking care of her two-year-old brother and two sisters (a four-year-old and an infant). Her mother said of her, "She looks small, but she can work like a big girl. When I go to work, she is responsible for feeding herself, her brother, and her sister. She also carries her four-month-old baby sister and feeds her milk with a spoon." While her mother was talking, Chinta came close to her father's lap and rubbed her head on his chest. He smiled at her approvingly.

Young untouchable boys, too, engage in domestic chores. During the agricultural season, ten-year-old Santosh Das, for example, cooked for and fed his two siblings while his parents were at work. When Santosh had to leave for cow herding, he left his siblings for a few hours with a neighbor. Because of these experiences, untouchable children from six to twelve years of age are much more mature and responsible than the same-aged high-caste children. At this age both boys and girls perform domestic chores, babysit, and herd cattle.

Untouchable girls not only help with domestic chores, but they are important contributors to family diet, as we noted in an earlier chapter. These girls have a much wider social radius than do high-caste girls, and they have a great deal of freedom of movement through their gathering and cow herding in pastures surrounding the village. The value of girls is repeatedly mentioned by parents, who appreciate their children's contribution to the family welfare. Hence one rarely sees special preference for a male child among the untouchables. Families may become concerned, however, if they do not have a son because sons can, among other things, become a *mahinder* and thereby ensure the contribution of one meal a day to the family. Sons can also inherit their fathers' contracts as *kirshan* or *bhagchasi.*

Sons are expected to live very close to their parents, but unlike high-caste families little stress is placed on the son's role in the perpetuation of the lineage. The Brahmanical ideology of a son's rights in patriarchal rites (e.g., funeral rites) is irrelevant in the social context of the untouchables. Also, unlike high-caste mothers, untouchable mothers do not expect to rule over subservient daughters-in-law. A daughter's departure from her parents' home after her marriage may not be a final one. Untouchable women maintain close contact with their parents throughout their lives, and they may return to their parent's home if the marriage does not work. It is not unusual for a wife's parents to live with her. Similarly, if food is scarce, a woman and her family may spend time at her parents' home. An untouchable girl learns to be self-reliant early in life. If she returns to her parents after a marital separation she is not seen as an economic burden, because she is able to work for her own living. Her male relatives almost always provide emotional support when her marriage breaks up.

Untouchable children have little spare time to play games, but they often turn their work time into play time. In the fields, boys play the flute and ride buffaloes; girls climb trees, play house, or chase each other's cows. Children of both sexes play with small balls, but while they enjoy these games they keep a careful eye on the livestock. During the agricultural season children have to watch the cows especially carefully so that they do not eat the crops.

Within the village, boys play separately from girls. Most of the time girls congregate in small groups to gather food or fuel; boys play with homemade carts or join wrestling games. Grown-ups encourage them in this competition. When they are in the fields children of both sexes play together, but when they quarrel they separate into boys' groups and girls' groups.

Untouchable children learn early in life that food cannot be taken for granted. Warmth and affection or harshness of treatment—whichever they experience at the hands of their parents—usually has something to do with work and with food. This reality of untouchable childhood is revealed in the following ethnographic sketches of individual children.

JUTHIKA LOHAR. Eleven-year-old Juthika woke up at six o'clock in the morning, just as her father was leaving for the field after his morning tea and puffed rice. Juthika's mother gave her raw tea mixed with jaggery and one biscuit. Juthika's younger sister had already had a biscuit and asked for another. The mother gave her a broken piece, and Juthika complained, "I want more too. Why did you give me less?" Her mother responded, "I can't give you any more."

After finishing her tea and biscuit she went outside and asked a girl from the neighbors' home, "Will you go outside and collect firewood with me?" But Juthika's mother cautioned, "You'd better come back on time to take rice to the field for your father. I don't need much fuel today." Around ten o'clock Juthika returned and took a bath. On her way out to take food to her father her mother said, "I have some extra rice here for you. Share the rice with your father. Don't eat too much, and see that your father eats well. He's working very hard now-a-days."

Juthika returned around noon and went to the field with eight cows and one buffalo. She returned home at four o'clock. After taking a bath she asked her mother, "Ma, could I have some puffed rice?" Her mother replied, "There is none in the house." So Juthika left home to play with her friends and returned at six o'clock saying, "Ma, I want some rice." Again her mother replied, "Can't you wait a little? Have you come after seeing a snake's feet?" (meaning, have you done something very great?). Juthika's father, who was sitting on the porch, interceded, saying, "Why don't you hurry up and give her some rice? Don't you realize she ate very little this morning?" He looked at Juthika lovingly, and Juthika returned his gaze. On another occasion, Juthika came home after gleaning paddy. Her mother looked very happy and said, "Store them carefully. When you have a lot, we will sell these to buy a shawl for you." Juthika asked, "Aren't you going to take the paddy away?" Smiling, her mother said, "No, I won't." And then she gave Juthika her meal.

MILAN LOHAR. At seven in the morning Milan's mother returned home after doing some domestic work in a Brahman home. Ten-year-old Milan was having tea with her father, and her mother said, "Milan, don't forget to wash the dishes." Milan went out to do as she was told, and when she returned she opened the end of her dress which was tucked into her waist and took out a bunch of mushrooms. Her mother looked very happy. She patted Milan's back and asked lovingly, "Where did you get so many mushrooms? They're so nice. We're going to have nice vegetables today." Milan left home at ten-thirty to take the cows to the field. The rice was not yet ready, so Milan left the house without eating anything, but later, around noon, her mother took her rice to the field where she was working. Milan returned home at four o'clock and took her little brother with her to play with some friends. When she came back, she said, "Ma, I'm so hungry." Her mother replied tenderly, "Yes, I know how hungry you are. I am late in getting the meal ready." She looked at a neighbor and continued, "I got so busy drying the paddy, I was late in cooking. My Milan is surely very hungry. All day long she was in the fields chasing the cows." Milan's mother then hurried to serve the meal just as Milan's father returned home from work. Milan gave her father a big smile and her father nodded warmly in return.

MANIK DAS. Seven-year-old Manik was having tea at seven o'clock in the morning. His father gave him puffed rice, and when Manik asked, "Can I have some more?" his father replied, "Not any more. There is none." Manik's mother spoke up, saying, "Why did you refuse to give him more?" She disappeared inside the room to get him more puffed rice. Later, at eleven o'clock, when Manik came home, his older sister served him fermented rice and told him to take the cows out. Manik's parents were both working in the field. At four Manik returned, took his bath and went out again. He returned at seven o'clock in the evening to have his meal. While he ate, he fed his brother and sister.

BHOKO HAZRA. At seven in the morning Bhoko's mother gave him and his brother tea and one biscuit each. After finishing his portion ten-year-old Bhoko said, "Ma, give me some of your tea." His mother complied and then said, "Bhoko, go to the fields where your father is working and get some snails." At eleven Bhoko ate his meal along with his father. After finishing, his father said, "Now you take the cows for herding." Bhoko retorted bluntly, "I won't." Angered by his resistance, Bhoko's father hit Bhoko a couple of times with a stick. Bhoko cried loudly and Bhoko's mother interceded, "Why don't you leave the cows near the house? I'll look after them." Bhoko complied and then went to play with his friends. He returned home in the evening to have a meal with his baby brother. After the meal Bhoko's mother instructed Bhoko, "Get me a matchbox from the store." Bhoko's mother then turned to her neighbor and continued her conversation, "I was very upset [at an earlier time]. I went to my parents and left the boys here, but they came to me after two days. They don't care for their father."

CHHABI HAZRA. Nine-year-old Chhabi came home at four o'clock in the afternoon, after selling for a rupee the paddy she had gleaned. Her mother demanded, "Give me the rupee." Chhabi refused saying, "I am going to the store. I won't give it to you." Angered, her mother retorted, "If you won't give it to me, I won't serve you any food." But Chhabi paid no attention and ran away to play with friends.

TAPATI DAS. When eleven-year-old Tapati returned from school she found her mother getting ready to visit her parents for three days. Tapati said, "I would like to go with you," but her father who was there said, "You have school. How can you miss three days?" Tapati became upset and locked herself in a room upstairs. "Come down immediately!" her father commanded. "If you don't, look at my hand. I have a stick. I shall beat you!" Tapati came down. The next morning her mother left with two of Tapati's younger siblings. Tapati was still upset when her grandmother said, "Tapati, get some firewood from the bush before you go to school." Tapati retorted, "I won't." Tapati's father came out of a room, saying, "You know very well how to swallow food without working for it. If you don't work, don't bother to eat!" Tapati left home that morning without eating, but she was given a piece of bread in the afternoon at school. When she returned home her aunt took her affectionately by the hand and led her to the kitchen where her grandmother served her a hot meal of rice. Tapati ate silently. "You must have been very hungry," her grandmother said. Tapati looked down shyly.

RAM HAZRA. Ten-year-old Ram did his school lessons early in the morning and went to the field for two hours to glean paddy. When he finished he ran home and gave the paddy to his mother, who smiled. Ram then ran to the pond for his bath, and when he returned his mother gave him some fermented rice. "Would you like some more?" she asked while he was eating. "No," he replied. "Take more," she urged. "You will be hungry at school." She gave him more which he ate silently.

JOYDEB LOHAR. Seven-year-old Joydeb's mother was a widow who worked in Santiniketan and had little time to look after her son. Joydeb's old grandmother was also a part-time domestic, so no one was home to feed the boy. Sometimes he went to his aunt and asked for food, but she ignored him. As a result, in the morning he often left without eating to herd the cows, sheep, and goats of a high-caste family. His grandmother came home around noon, however, and gave him fermented rice. At four o'clock Joydeb returned from the field and went to play with friends, and at night—around eight o'clock—he ate dinner. One night while having his meal Joydeb told his mother, "I would like some more vegetable curry." But his mother said, "No more for you." Joydeb started to cry and his mother slapped him. Joydeb cried for a while longer and then finished what he had not eaten. His mother said, "The bed is ready. You go to sleep!" Joydeb's neighbors complained about this mother's negligence. The mother herself, however, was experiencing major hardships working as a domestic and trying to provide money for her son's food. She spent the whole day at work and returned home exhausted in the evening. Eventually Joydeb was appointed a *mahinder* in a high-caste home, and his neighbors, who gave the boy food whenever they could, were happy for him. "Now the boy will eat well," they said.

Adolescence to Adulthood among Untouchables

The transition to manhood for untouchable males is recognized when youths learn to handle a plow. Until then, youngsters of both sexes are involved in virtually the same economic activities. A twenty-year-old Baen man told this story about learning to use a plow:

> When I was a boy I used to attend Palashpur school. There were very few of our kind there. I did not feel comfortable playing with Brahman boys, though they were nice to me. I used to skip school and visit my father and elder brothers while they plowed in the fields. One day my father said, "Come and try this." I was very happy. I tried, but it was very heavy. Anyway, I just loved helping my father and brothers. When they asked me to go to school, I cried to my mother, "I want to learn to cultivate. I do not want to go to school." After some days, I finally learned to work with the plow.

At adolescence, many untouchable males travel outside the village to work at road construction, digging, or even as *nagda chashi* for landowners elsewhere. From this time onward they earn more wages than women, and their work world becomes much wider than before. But they also confront an urban world in which they must compete with other men struggling to get jobs.

After menarche, untouchable females usually stop cow herding alone outside the village. These young women now accompany older women to the fields and help transplant during the growing season. A twenty-four-year-old Lohar woman recounted, "I became a woman in my thirteenth year. My mother no longer allowed me to go far into the pastures, so I followed her to the rice fields. Previously she took me only to cut grass, but this time she found a transplanting job for me. I was very happy to earn so much money and to be able to work like other women."

The contrast in physical appearance between the richer high-caste women and poor untouchable women in Palashpur is striking. Untouchable women are usually healthy looking, with clear skin and lustrous hair. In comparison, high-caste women look somewhat pale. In spite of their poverty, untouchable women eat nutritious foods such as small fresh fish, snails and conches, freshly picked greens, and fermented rice and fermented palm wine or rice beer—which constitutes a fairly balanced diet. Ironically, even though high-caste women eat more rice they do not have the regular supply of small fish, fresh greens, or vitamin-rich fermented rice, which is considered "poor man's" food.[10] Also, the work life of untouchable women seems more rewarding, and the longer hours of outdoor physical activity seems to be healthful. Within the village, untouchable teenage girls handle large round nets used for fishing in the community ponds. They also sell fish, crabs, and snails from door to door. It is not unusual to see two or three young women—married or unmarried—walking along a village path carrying the huge nets over their shoulders.

Young untouchable women usually marry at fifteen or sixteen. As in high-caste families, their marriages are typically arranged by kinsmen, but unlike high-caste girls, these young women sometimes save money to buy new clothing for their own wedding. Since untouchable men, who typically marry around twenty or twenty-one, are not expected to fully support their wives after marriage, young untouchable brides carry on their own economic activities, thereby giving them more independence as wives than their high-caste counterparts (see Ullrich 1977).

Husbands and Wives in High-Caste Families

A new wife in a high-caste family is expected to be demure, subservient, and quiet. For the first few years of her married life, and certainly until she bears a child (preferably a boy), she lives a subdued existence in her husband's extended or joint family. Increasingly, however, newly married wives in Palashpur are failing to honor the traditional norms of being the submissive daughter-in-law. Older people, especially mothers-in-law, lament the new change. Almost all these older women recall how they displayed in their own youth an "ideal obedience" toward their domineering mothers-in-law. Now they complain, "Young girls are too arrogant. They charm their husbands and disobey their elders." Yet the norm remains that a "good son" gives priority to his mother over his wife (see also Roy 1975; Seymour 1975).

10. See chap. 7 for information about caste differences in food consumption among children in two nearby villages.

Ideally, a wife should regard her husband as her lord. In reality, very few wives believe this. Nonetheless, most high-caste wives conform to the social etiquette of outward passivity. Several young men indicated they would like to have their wives as companions and friends, but few couples have either the means or the liberty to enjoy doing things together. And the expected polarity of sexes is so distinct in Palashpur that couples have very little opportunity to interact socially. In the domestic sphere young men are expected to act with restraint, without showing outward affection toward their wives. Such expressive behavior would be offensive to the elders and shameful to the children. Lack of privacy separates the couple during the day. However, in spite of social restrictions, young women are usually happy after marriage, which was a cherished dream during the monotony of their unmarried life. Young wives frequently complain about their in-laws, but none of the sample wives felt negative about their husbands.

When a newly married daughter returns for a visit to her parents in Palashpur, she is usually proud of her transition in status. She wears bright *sindur*—sometimes a little too much in the part of her hair—and she wears shining gold jewelry and a bright red sari received as a wedding gift from her relatives. Some girls are eager to talk to their friends about their husbands, but they are often bashful in front of elders. Young wives are often critical of the women in-laws in their new home, though overtly they express an attitude of deference to them. After a few years of marriage, especially if a woman becomes a mother, she may talk back to her mother-in-law and sister-in-law. The idealized image of a subjugated, demure daughter-in-law found in many works of Indian anthropology is seldom a true reflection of women's actual behavior within the family. As a woman matures she gradually gains a stronger position within her husband's family. Her sisters-in-law get married, one by one, and the presence of her husband's younger brother's new wife gives her a superior position as the elder brother's wife. Moreover, as the mother-in-law gets older she shifts the responsibility of the household to her daughters-in-law. By the time a woman reaches middle age, she often becomes more dominant within the household than her husband. Thus even though her husband holds formal authority, she often comes to control the family with informal power.

Exposure to the outside world is restricted for both married and unmarried high-caste women. The little experience they have with the outside world comes from making annual visits to their parents' homes, attending occasional movies or community feasts for weddings or funerals, watching all-night *jatra* theater during Dharmapuja, described at greater length in chapter 5, or visiting temples within a few miles of Palashpur. Women never travel alone, but after they get older they may venture alone into the neighborhood. Young high-caste women who have been married for as long as five or six years, however, often know no one in the community. The only men they speak to are their husbands, husbands' younger brothers, their age-mates, and their fathers-in-law. All other men must be avoided.

Mature high-caste men do not stay home during the day. Rather, they leave the village for shopping, visiting friends and relatives, or going to movies. Attending political meetings is also a frequent diversion in the idle life-style of high-caste men. All twenty high-caste men between the ages of thirty-eight and sixty-five who were interviewed in this research felt that the best years of their lives were before they married. At that time they enjoyed considerable status within their families because of their potential for earning a salary or bringing in substantial dowry. Now economic pressures brought about by the high cost of living, the burden of having to pay dowry for their own daughters, and the unemployment of their sons worry them.

All these men expect to be taken care of in old age by their sons. Another old but childless couple in the village said they expect their nephews to take care of them. Their expectation is fully appropriate because younger people—even unrelated neighbors—are expected to help care for the aged in Palashpur. Children are advised repeatedly to be respectful to elders and to look after the old. Older siblings are also taught to be responsible for younger siblings, while the latter are taught to be obedient to their elders. Even daughters-in-law who have been oppressed earlier by domineering mothers-in-law generally do not ignore or neglect their aging mothers-in-law. As grandparents, aging men and women tend to be indulgent toward children, and many children become closer to their grandmothers than to their own mothers, especially if their mothers have other smaller children to tend.

Husbands and wives become closer as they mature and have the opportunity to share more of daily family life. Wives are often deferential to husbands, but they also often manage the family finances and make influential decisions about the selection of a spouse for their children. For example, children frequently take their mothers into their confidence to express opinions about a prospective spouse, and mothers convey the youths' sentiments back to their husbands, sometimes in masked form. Over time women become increasingly domineering within the family, and men often become noninterfering in everyday family matters. Thus, middle-aged or older fathers frequently appear to have peripheral positions within the family. Older widowed women also hold superior ritual status within the family because of the purity of their life-style, a purity that allows them ideally to become caretakers of the family shrine. If no older woman resides in the household, the wife or a daughter assumes this religious responsibility. Moreover, mothers and grandmothers together offer basic religious training to children and they teach offspring important caste rules such as the need to bathe after touching a low-caste person (cf. Carstairs 1957, 148–49).

Marital separation is rare even in unhappy high-caste families. Conflict between spouses arises for a variety of reasons, such as a husband's excessive drinking or his spending family money on wine and women. In Palashpur, husbands were not drunkards in only two of the eleven extremely unhappy marriages in which the wives were battered. In one of these cases the wife refused to sell land (which she had received from her father) to meet her husband's sister's dowry. In the other case the husband became suspicious that his wife was having an affair with his elder brother. Villagers deplore wife battering, but often the wives themselves suffer abuse quietly in order to hide the shame. Only four of the eleven battered women drew attention to the abuse by screaming or by coming out of their houses and cursing their husbands. One fifty-year-old husband was beaten by his sons for beating their mother.

Interviews with both happy and unhappy wives showed women's disdain for men who attempt to hurt their wives physically. Men too tended to express distaste for such husbands, but when asked whether the battered wives should seek a divorce all the men said no. In general, villagers agree that it is very bad for a husband to mistreat his wife and to behave like an "uncultured" person. Still, a wife must not leave her husband, "because a husband is her superior, like a lord to a woman." After some probing, high-caste women admitted, "Anyway, where can a high-caste woman go after a divorce?"

Husbands and Wives in Untouchable Families

Ideologically, husbands in untouchable marriages also hold superior status over their wives, but in happy households husbands and wives share a more equal companionship. Untouchable men share such household chores as cooking, cleaning, washing, and caring for babies. From childhood onward, men are socialized to perform these chores along with women. Men and women also enjoy drinking together. During festival times such as Dharmapuja, for example, men and women participate in all-night festivities. During Bhajo worship (an untouchable festival described in chap. 5), men play drums and gongs while women dance. Men and women tease each other with rhymes composed by women. The entire family joins the merrymaking. Women brew rice wine, and entertain men and women guests. However, the women are careful to observe proper social behavior with unrelated men.

A new untouchable wife starting married life and work for the first time in Palashpur is often diffident around other villagers, who are strangers to her. Even though she goes to work in the fields each day with other untouchable wives, she often feels constrained in her social life for the first two or three years. Gradually, as these wives get to know each other, they move about the village more comfortably. New wives also get to know the outside world by accompanying other women who seek jobs elsewhere. The economic partnership between untouchable wives and husbands, along with their mutual dependencies, helps make their conjugal relationship a satisfying one. Harmonious marital relationships cannot be taken for granted however. A husband's irresponsible behavior or a wife's defiance of her husband's authority creates tensions in the marital relationship. Wife beating is no secret in untouchable homes. For example, a husband may demand money from the wife's earnings. If the wife refuses to give her husband money, she may be beaten. In retaliation, a wife might stop cooking, shout abuses, fight back, or sometimes leave the husband, taking the dowry and children with her. Much less shame is attached to this kind of conflict among untouchables than in high-caste families, and unlike high-caste wives, untouchable wives complain openly about their husbands' behavior.

Despite the greater freedom experienced by untouchable wives than by high-caste wives, local cultural ideology sustains the belief in the husband's superior standing over the wife. Also, untouchables tend to share the sentiment that the husband is like a guardian to his wife, and if a wife misbehaves the husband has the right to discipline her. In day-to-day behavior, though, the great majority of untouchable wives defy their husbands by walking out on them, especially if the wives are still young. The following are three cases of conjugal tension where the self-reliance of untouchable wives is revealed.

CASE 1. Late one afternoon during the agricultural season a Handi husband said peremptorily to his wife, "Prepare a nice vegetable with fresh snails. I want to have it with my wine," His wife retorted, "I've been transplanting all day, and I'm very tired. I can't cook now." Her husband yelled, "You must prepare this!" "I don't care if you drink or not," she yelled back, "I'm not going to cook it for you!" Furious, her husband beat her with a bamboo stick. His wife screamed, "How dare you hit me like this. I shall never go to work again!" He shouted, "I am going to marry another wife." But she scoffed, saying, "Your ass splits to feed one wife and you brag about marrying another one!" She did not cook that night, but she did continue transplanting the next morning.

CASE 2. A Baen daily-wage earner came home without having found a job that day, but his wife had earned money working on road construction. "Give me some money for my drink," he demanded. "We need money for food," she cautioned, and continued, "Don't you realize we also have two children to feed?" Her husband shouted, "You give me at least a rupee!" But his wife refused. The man became furious and thrashed her as she ran screaming from the house, "I curse you to be a cow to be killed by a Muslim! I curse you to be a pig to be killed by the Santal! You are not worthy of being a human being or a father of children!"

CASE 3. A Lohar wife received her monthly pay of five rupees (about 63 cents) for working as a domestic. But her husband took the money without asking, to drink with his friends. When his wife found out she shouted, "You, the beef-eater! You steal my money for your drink. You should be ashamed to be a man." Angered by this verbal abuse the husband began to beat her, but a young man interfered and stopped the fight. The next morning the wife left her husband.

The main reason for such marital conflict among untouchables is the wife's perception of the husband's behavior as "irresponsible." Women often criticize men with sarcastic remarks such as, "There is no food in your stomach or the stomachs of your children and yet you fill your empty stomach with liquor." Sometimes the women fight back physically: "If he beats her once, she beats him twice." Women with older children, however, rarely leave their husbands because, as one said, "I am the mother of three. If I go, it would be too much of a burden on my parents."

Untouchable men seem to have a much harder time than women coping with crushing poverty and with the unpredictability of their future. Moreover, men are also often exposed to an unfriendly world of urban unemployment which they must face alone, without the secure context of their identity as a member of a family and community. An untouchable woman, on the other hand, seldom approaches her urban employer alone, and she is rarely addressed by her first name. Rather, she is addressed as somebody's daughter, wife, or mother, indicating her belonging in a social group. Men, however, remain alone to confront an insensitive world that offers them only an untouchable status and barely helps them meet their responsibilities as "men of the family."

Perhaps for reasons such as these many untouchable men look sickly after they pass the age of thirty, even though women give them the best food. The Brahmanic ideology of male superiority probably exacerbates the feelings of hopelessness. That is, since untouchable men live in close association with high-caste men, it is difficult to escape entirely the Brahmanic ideology that asserts a man is "Lord of his household." In reality, none of these untouchable men can be "Lord" of their households without help from their wives and children. So even though a bottle of toddy may not fill their stomachs, it may help them forget temporarily the hunger at home.

CHAPTER 5

Religious Beliefs: Festivals and Rituals

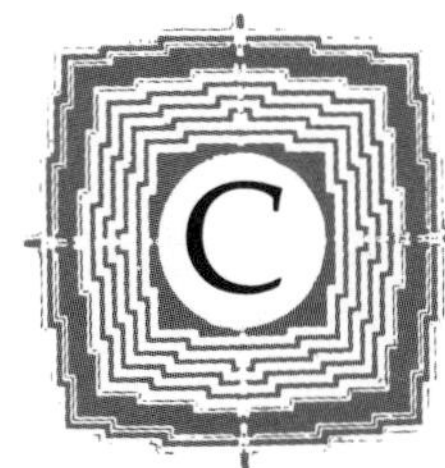

hildren in Palashpur grow up in an environment rich with religious festivals and rituals. They do not receive formal religious teaching within a structured framework, but by being continuously exposed to and participating in community festivals, worships, and family rituals they gradually form their beliefs about the supernatural world. Though different castes observe these festivities and worships in different ways, the rituals appear to satisfy the needs of all caste groups.

Religious practices in Palashpur may be studied in two broad contexts, namely, the community and the family. With the exception of the Bhajo festival described later, community rituals tend to be a male domain, with women entering only at the periphery. But in family rituals women have the central role. A Bengali Hindu child gains religious faith through constant exposure to these two domains, both of which are suffused with an aura of Mother worship.[1]

1. Unlike Christianity, Judaism, or Islam, Hinduism has no paramount male authority. The religious scriptures and the so called high-traditional philosophy are, however, strongly male as well as Brahman dominated. In fact, these religious texts were originally inaccessible to non-Brahmans and to women. The source of religion for non-Brahmans was folklore, mythology, and the legends of

Community Ritual: A Male-Dominated Domain

Being a Brahman-dominated village, non-Brahmans in Palashpur are excluded from traditional Hindu temples. The eleven temples in Palashpur dedicated to Hindu male and female deities belong to Brahman households, with daily family worship. Larger worships occur on auspicious occasions. Not only are Brahmans alone allowed to worship in these temples, but only they may dedicate flower offerings.[2] Other castes may offer whole fruit and money to the Brahman priest, who then dedicates these on their behalf. Some temple priests have clientele from distant villages. On certain annual worships both high-caste and untouchable devotees arrive with their gifts to be dedicated by the priest to the temple deities. Some of these temples organize special celebrations during September and October to worship Mother Durga (the goddess of strength) and Mother Kali (the destroyer of evil). Images are especially made by the local Chhutor craftsmen, and Baen drummers are engaged for drumming and beating the gongs. A Brahman priest sacrifices goats to observe the ritual and to receive *prasad,* the food that has been offered to the deity.

The four-day Durgapuja (i.e, Durga worship) is the most important festival in West Bengal. People expect to wear new clothes, repair and clean their houses, visit each other, entertain, and be entertained during this period. Durgapuja is not as grand in Palashpur as Dharmapuja, but there is much merrymaking, especially among children. Immediately after Durgapuja every high-caste home observes Laxmipuja (i.e., worship of the goddess of prosperity). Two Laxmi images are worshiped in the temples for the community on the evening of a full moon. After

---

two great religious epics, the Ramayana and Mahabharata. These were acted, recited, danced, painted, and expressed in all possible media throughout India. Examples from these epics are cited in everyday conversation as the ideals of a son, daughter, wife, mother, and others.

2. Elsewhere in West Bengal, non-Brahman high castes are allowed to make these flower offerings. Many non-Brahman residents of Palashpur, for example, visit temples in the nearby town of Bolpur to make their offerings.

a fortnight—with the appearance of a new moon—comes Kalipuja, the worship of Mother Kali, and Deepa *bali,* the festival of lights. Five Kali worships are recognized in Palashpur, two in Brahman temples and three for the community as a whole. Villagers gather at an ancient spot beneath a banyan tree to offer their gifts to Mother Kali, and people sometimes vow to sacrifice goats for the diety. The Brahman priest of Kali *tala* organizes a community feast with donations from the villagers.

In recent years two youth organizations have organized two separate community worships of Kali, with contributions from the villagers and from residents of surrounding areas. In these worships, non-Brahman high castes are allowed to offer flowers to the deity, but untouchables are still excluded from this privilege. All castes contribute money, rice, and vegetables for a large community feast, which is cooked by local Brahmans. Young men and children enjoy the festival days by setting off firecrackers and fireworks.

Another important celebration is the worship of the goddess of wisdom and art (i.e., Saraswatipuja), which is performed by schoolchildren in the month of January. In addition to these worships in homes and temples, a community worship for Saraswati is held on the school premises. Schoolchildren fast until the offering of flowers is made, and they place their books near the image of the goddess and write her name ("I bow to Saraswati") three times on each book. Their invocation and prayers are believed to bring success in learning and good grades on the examination. Untouchable students do not attend the invocation and prayers.

Bengali religious beliefs emphasize the divinity associated with *shakti,* the feminine expression or power of the Supreme Being, Mother Durga. The goddess Durga is depicted as a mature woman astride a lion while slaying the buffalo demon, a symbol of violent and evil power. The buffalo demon is shown as a muscular man with a thick mustache and hairy chest. His chest is pierced by the Mother's trident. With a tender and compassionate expression, she holds ten weapons in her ten hands. Mother Durga is customarily shown with four other dieties: (*a*) Laxmi the goddess of prosperity and grace), pictured as a young married woman with an owl; (*b*) Ganesha (the god of business and success, and god of the common people), the elephant-headed god with a mouse; (*c*) Saraswati (the goddess of art and wisdom), depicted as a young unmarried woman sitting on a swan; and (*d*) Kartikeya (the god of war), shown as a handsome bachelor riding a peacock. Together these five gods and goddesses form a family, the latter four being Durga's children. Siva is painted as a yogi at the top of the depiction, in the background. The images are made of straw, plastered with clay, and then painted and decorated with silk and jewelry. Each image exhibits the traditional art of clay image-making.

To most people in Bengali society, and in folklore, Mother Durga is viewed as the married daughter who returns to her parents along with her children for only a few days. After four days and nights of worship, the images are immersed in the river. Mother Durga then returns to her husband's (Siva's) abode in the Kailasha Mountain in the Himalayas. An important aspect of this ritual is the recitation of 108 verses of the religious text dedicated to Durga. Each verse asks for a very practical blessing from the Mother, for example, wealth, wisdom, good health, a handsome spouse, victory over one's enemies, and so forth. The chanting is done in simple Sanskrit with Bengali pronunciation. The verses also describe Durga in such terms as "the Mother," "a nurse," "the strength," "wisdom," and "wealth."

The association of Mother worship with earthly mothers and daughters is a significant part of the social values in Palashpur. Motherhood is often associated with a divine aura, and femininity is frequently recognized as a spiritual power needed for devotion to god. The teaching of the Sanskrit text "your mother and motherland are greater than heaven" became a popular political slogan during the struggle for independence in nineteenth- and twentieth-century India. A related aphorism states, "your mother is the greatest on this earth; your father is the greatest in heaven." Children internalize this ideology in the course of their socialization and rarely make negative statements about their mothers in public. Children's achievements are often referred to as their mothers' achievements. If a child escapes a danger, for example, someone might remark, "Look at the strength of his mother's milk." But by the same token, mothers are made responsible for wayward children.

While most mother images in West Bengal are fashioned like beautiful women, the image of Mother Kali is shown as a woman garlanded with human heads, wearing a skirt of human hands, holding swords with blood stains. With one foot she steps over the bosom of Lord Siva, who lies supine. This horrifying image of Mother Kali—as the destroyer of evil—has often generated confusion among foreign scholars. Carstairs (1957), for example, used Mother Kali to create a psychoanalytic metaphor explaining a child's association of a dominant and overpowering mother with her bloodstained clothes (during menstruation), causing in the child an inner horror and fear of violence—all sublimating into the divine image of "Mother and protectress" and "Mother the terrifying."

In contrast to this Western interpretation, most villagers themselves hold the explanation described below, which is handed down to them through local folklore and ballads. Mother Kali is depicted alternatively as a mischievous daughter and as a loving mother who has to wear the most horrifying appearances to crush the powerful Asura—the embodiment of evil and beastly power. Siva lying on the floor is often explained in West Bengal as follows: Mother Kali had to appear as the most horrifying one. She is seen first as Durga killing Mahisharma, the buffalo demon. Then she attacked the Asura called Raktabeeja (i.e., "offspring who emanate from every drop of blood"), but Raktabeeja created thousands of violent Asuras. When these demons challenged her she became furious. From the black of her eyes came Kali, the embodiment of the destructive power of Mother Kali. She killed the demons one after another. Eventually she became completely engrossed in war, but it was time to stop, so Siva—her husband and the symbol of peace—lay on the ground. When she stepped over him she became embarrassed and "stuck out her tongue" (a common Bengali expression of feeling embarrassed) and became still.

Goddesses in West Bengal are addressed as mother or daughter, revealing the spiritual aura of femininity that pervades much of the religious faith in the male domain. All these Mother worships are backed by Hindu Sanskritic scripture and are founded on a higher-order Brahmanic philosophy.[3] Festivals are shared by Bengali Hindus throughout India and abroad, wherever a large Bengali community exists.

Palashpur religious life shows a distinctive feature found perhaps only in the Birbhum district of West Bengal, namely, the festival of Dharmapuja. Palashpur has a special status in the realm of this celebration because the annual Dharmaraj worship begins in Palashpur on the full moon of the Bengali month Chaitra (between March and April) and is later followed by many other villages in Birbhum. Scholars of Bengali culture have found conflicting evidence regarding the location of the origin of the festival, but all agree that it had an indigenous origin among the untouchables of Bengal (Mitra 1972). In his extensive study of Dharmapuja, Mitra and other scholars (Sengupta 1955) confirm the strong expression of non-Brahmanic features, the use of rice wine, a series of rituals of self-torture, and pig sacrifice as the characteristics of autochthonous culture.

Traditionally the priests of Dharmapuja were untouchable Handis or Doms. At one time in Palashpur a Napit officiated as priest, but over the past seventy years the priesthood has shifted first to an Adhikari Brahman (a Brahman of lower rank) and later to a Bhatacharyya Brahman. Still, in certain rituals, Handi and non-Brahman touchable castes are needed to officiate as priests. The three-day-and-night festival indicates the pervasive importance of the untouchable community. The Brahmanic ritual procedure is followed, along with long Bengalized Sanskrit denoting a divine male as the supreme deity without any form. The

3. Hindu religious history (Sen 1948; Haldar 1954) shows a continuous compromise between mother-centered religious beliefs and male-centered religious ideologies. Pre-Aryan culture of the Indus Valley during the second and third millennia B.C. shows evidence of two clear trends in people's religious life—worship of fertility goddesses by the common people and a priest-dominated mystical concept. Later in Indian history the Aryans introduced a strongly male-centered religious trend. The pre-Aryan goddesses did not vanish (Piggot 1960). Rather they kept their original forms, and some were gradually developed into mother images. Aryan gods were placed as husbands of these goddesses. Gradually high intellectual metaphysics developed with the concept of Supreme Mother. The male counterparts are looked upon as holding a superior status to the females, but the omnipotent power of the Mother is believed to supersede all male deities in the eastern part of India, including West Bengal.

verses are recited to support Dharma's Brahmanic (i.e., high-caste) origin. Dharmaraj is called Banesvar (which is another name for the Brahmanic deity, Siva), symbolized, as we observed in chapter 3, by a four-foot phallic-shaped wooden pole with fresh flowers and fruit nailed to it. The pole is also painted red with *sindur.* Banesvar is carried to every house of the village except the Baen.

There is no image for Dharmaraj, but white-painted clay horses indicate Dharmaraj's presence. The unseen presence of the deity is shown by an empty spot on the altar surrounded by several stones representing Dharmaraj's emissaries such as Chandrai, Kalurai, and Meghrai. These three male divinities are deified forms of three legendary heroes from the Dom caste who served as commanders-in-chief of the army of past rulers of the region. Their bravery and heroic deeds were perceived as manifestations of divine powers. Untouchable men dedicate themselves as special devotees to the ritual (i.e., as *bhaktyas*) and go through painful ordeals to participate in the rituals. For example, they walk on burning embers, whip each other, press thorns over their breasts, and hang by their legs while swinging over an open fire. The Baen are not allowed to be *bhaktya,* but no ritual can be performed without their playing the huge drums called *dhaks.*

Untouchable women also participate as *bhaktya,*but they go through a different set of physical penances. One important ritual for them occurs in the middle of the night when they take a bath in the holy pond, Muktadhar, on the outskirts of the village. Lying face down, they then crawl on their breasts to the temple. Alternatively, they may walk to the temple with an earthen pot of burning charcoal on their head. Large numbers of drummers follow these women in a procession, accompanied by hundreds of other men, women, and children. Women *bhaktyas* are called *mahamila,* meaning "the great women." Dharmaraj is the bestower of boons, especially rain, children, and good crops. Untouchables take vows to become *bhaktya* (male devotees) or *mahamila* (female devotees), and high-caste men and women usually vow to feast the poor or to sacrifice goats or sheep for Dharmaraj. Untouchables also vow to sacrifice goats and pigs.

These complex rituals take place over three days and nights, and they involve nearly the entire village and its surrounding area. On the last day, drummers circle exuberantly near the holy spot of Meghrai, on the southwestern outskirts of the village. This ritual, called "the roar of thunder," glorifies Meghrai, the Lord of the Clouds. As we noted in chapter 3, this ritual is usually followed by hundreds of drummers and men dancing as if intoxicated, while *bhaktyas* carrying holy pots of rice wine walk through the village street to the holy pond on the eastern outskirt of the village. Men, women, and children follow them. Amidst ear-piercing drumbeating and excited spectators, Brahmans sacrifice goats and sheep at a holy spot called Burorai, which is believed to be the place of origin of the deity. A Handi priest sacrifices a pig. In the meantime a *bhaktya* walks into the pond and stands in water up to his neck. He carries with him the ritual pot of rice wine. Another *bhaktya* then carries the pig's head into the water. He places the head in the pot of wine, and pushes the pot and its carrier under water. As the pot sinks, the men swim to shore, and the pond water is sprinkled over the spectators. Many people press close to the *bhaktyas* to receive the water that is believed to purify their bodies. As the sun sets the festival ends.

Persons familiar with Hindu Brahmanic ritual readily recognize the unusual character of this ritual with its synchronism of Brahmanic and non-Brahmanic elements. Many Hindu festivals show blends of the two sets of traits (see, for example, Marriott 1955), but perhaps none in Bengal show such distinctively different characteristics side by side. Moreover, overt prominence of the untouchable sector of the community is unusual in rituals officiated by a Brahman priest.

An eighty-year-old Brahman man described Dharmaraj *puja* as follows: "Originally, it belonged to the untouchables only, but gradually Brahmans recognized the great power of Dharmaraj and the efficacy of his worship. So they accepted the *puja*. In the beginning there was no Brahman *bhaktya;* only an untouchable could endure such physical pain. Nowadays one notices a few Brahmans taking this vow." A Dom woman continued, "Dharmapuja belongs to the Dom. It is our *puja*. Because the deity is so great, the Brahmans wanted to worship him." This woman's husband was a *bhaktya*. She told how careful she must be about serving her husband food with uncooked flour, fruit, milk, and jaggery—all typically Brahmanic foods used for ritual purity. Menstruating women may not touch this food, and strict celibacy is required for both men and women participating in the ritual. All of these acts are part of the Brahmanic prescription for ritual purity.

On another occasion a Lohar *bhaktya* asserted, "During these days I become equal to a Brahman." He then showed a white sacred thread that was given to him by a Brahman at the beginning of the festival after the *bhaktya* had taken a ritual bath in the holy pond to release him from bondage. During the ritual, however, Brahman priests affirm their superiority by walking over the shoulders of the *bhaktyas,* who bow to the ground. At the end of the festival men from all castes embrace each other. The sacred thread of the *bhaktyas* is then thrown into the holy pond, and untouchable men return to their lowly status. The Brahman priest performs a purifying ritual for Dharmaraj, who has been contaminated by coming into physical contact with the untouchables, and he performs his daily worship at the temple. Non-Brahmans are not allowed into the shrine room until the next year's festival. Traditional caste distinctions are thus continued after a brief relaxation of rules. The Brahman accepts a non-Brahman deity, but he maintains his distance from the untouchables by introducing the purification ritual—not only for the Brahman, but also for the deity.

Two community festivals not dominated by Brahman authority are the festival of the snake goddess (Manasha) and of the rain goddess (Bhajo). The goddess Manasha is a lesser deity identified with Siva's wife.[4] During the Bengali month of Bhadra (July–August), at the peak of the rainy season, the Lohar celebrate an all-night worship of Manasha. Men, women, and children throughout the untouchable sector of the community join the feasting and wine drinking. They gather in front of a pitcher of water—symbolizing the deity—beneath the thatched roof of a tiny cottage. Men and women participate in the ritual on an

4. In Palashpur during the rainy season, another image of the snake goddess, Chintamoni, is brought from a nearby town for worship at the Dharmaraj temple. The image is carried by people of the Napit caste, and it is worshiped by the Brahmans. No festival is attached to it, and only high-caste people offer money and rice to the image.

equal basis. One man and one woman carry the holy pitcher and lead a procession in song invoking the goddess Manasha. Baen drummers follow them. Men often stop the procession and recite verses with the following refrain, "Oh, brother, listen to me." The theme song continues:

> Oh, Mother Manasha.
> Oh, Mother Kamala [one who sits on a lotus].[5]
> Come out of the water.
> Step on the lotus.
> Come onto the bank of the pond.
> Oh, Mother, bestow your blessings upon us.

Occasionally women go into a trance and speak as if the goddess herself were talking through them. Once, for example, a woman spoke about the cause of her granddaughter's illness. The processioners listened to her carefully and then sprinkled water on her to bring her back to her senses.

The processioners march to a pond, where the pitcher is filled with water and brought back to the holy hut. After the worship has been completed, men and women drink heavily and feast on sacrificial goat meat. Children participate in all of these festivities throughout the night. Although the members of the Lohar community collect food and money from all high-caste homes to support the ritual, none of the high-caste people themselves participate in the festival, except for a few men who come as curious spectators.

The Bhajo festival on the last day of the Bengali month Bhadra is basically an untouchable women's festival, though Baen men as drummers must also be present to accompany the songs and dances. Women describe Bhajo as Lord Indra, a Vedic god of rain, but in Palashpur Bhajo is depicted physically as a married woman in a typical red-bordered white sari. A small banana plant is wrapped and shaped into the image of a woman. The shrine for her is placed inside the bush made of green herbal leaves and plantain plants. The deity is surrounded by thirteen different earth pots of sprouted grain and decorated with long

5. Kamala is another name for Laxmi.

stalks of water lilies, all signifying a fertility rite celebrating the fecundity of women and earth.

In the evening women go to the pond singing,

> Oh, Mother. Oh, beautiful Bhajo.
> Oh, the goddess, our Mother.
> Come and help us celebrate.

The drummers follow them. Baen women of all ages, including young girls of ten or eleven, fast all day and carry water pots to the pond. While they fill the pots, some of the women and girls go into trance. Other women support them back to the shrine. On their way, several women generally start shaking to the drum beat and go into trance. After reaching the shrine, these women begin to speak out while still in trance, and they shake violently almost as if in a rage. Some cry loudly, complaining about their family conflicts. People respect these words as if they were the words of Bhajo herself. After being comforted, these women come out of their possessed state and appear exhausted. Following a period of rest they break their fast with puffed rice and wine.

Women worship Bhajo in Bengali verses and dance all night to the cadence of male drummers. There is considerable teasing in these verses, some of which would be improper in everyday social settings. Women, for example, talk provocatively about married men and women having illicit affairs, and women tease the men. The men answer in mock anger through vigorous drumming and dancing. Young Baen boys join their elders throughout the night, carrying and playing small drums. After the all-night festival, women walk to the rice fields and throw arrows into the corners to protect the crop. They then fetch green paddy and pick flowers to distribute in all the untouchable homes. The festival is followed the next day by a community feast, prepared by men as well as women.

In Bhajo, the possession of women and the rebellious protest against social problems are similar to possession states elsewhere in which possession is interpreted as feminine protest against social oppression in a male-dominated society. Given their inferior position in the caste hierarchy and their sociostructural inferiority to men, it seems plausible that the protest of Baen women in this safe, ritual context is a way of venting frustration and hostility against the social system. Teasing between the sexes also reminds one of a mild sex-war.

Each year in April high-caste men organize a communal feast so that all castes may celebrate the worship of Dhanika Chandi (another name for Durga), the mother goddess who is the guardian deity of Palashpur's cremation ground. No material image is created for this worship. A priest simply performs the ritual at a mound of stone, as the representation of the deity.

All these community festivals, except Dharmapuja, glorify the mother image of God. This fact provides a suggestive lead for the study of children in Palashpur, as we amplify later. We should also note that Dharmaraj, though perceived as a male deity, is not represented with any visual aura of maleness except in the symbolic figure of Banesvar. Banesvar's phallic shape and association with fruit and flowers suggest the male physiological priority in procreation. Also, following Victor Turner (1969), one might associate Dharmaraj's white horse with the representation of male virility and the vermillion paste painted over Banesvar as the symbol of menstrual fluid, the source of fecundity. Hence, both sexes may be recognized intrinsically.

Dharmaraj *puja* also plays a significant role in the control of Palashpur's rigid caste hierarchy. The participants in the core rituals are untouchable men and women. Here the ritual penances may be seen as a therapeutic performance for the socially oppressed. The words of the old Brahman, "Only an untouchable could endure such physical pain," is significant in this social context. Like the male *bhaktyas,* female *mahamilas* find an opportunity to gain a temporary high status by going through painful penance. Brahmans feel no need to go through such ordeals.

Community rituals among the untouchables do not show the same separation of sexes as in the Brahmanic rituals such as Durgapuja, Kalipuja, and others. In the Manasha festival, both sexes participate in the core ritual of invocation of Manasha, as well as in the collective celebration. Similarly, even though Bhajo is a woman's ritual, men participate to support the festivities, whereas in the Brahmanic festivals one finds a strict separation of sexes. Women join these as spectators only or sometimes as helpers in the preparation of a feast, but not in cooking.

Family Rituals: A Female-Dominated Domain

Focus on family rituals helps one to correlate the spirituality of motherhood in a male-oriented social structure with the religious life of the people. The life-cycle rituals such as the sacred thread rites (*upanayana*), wedding rites, and funeral rites all follow patriarchal procedures, with a preponderance of males participating in the core rituals. All of these rituals confirm the value of the patrilineage and the sociostructural superiority of males. But during all these rituals women take an active part in the social activities. In a series of so-called women's rituals, women in groups—especially at weddings—assert their social position in Hindu society. None of these rituals are recognized in Brahmanic ritual order, and none follow any prescribed text. But they do have a systematic repertoire handed down through generations of women. Most of the rituals deal with sexual potency, fertility, and harmony in conjugal relationships. In fact, often the "women's rituals" are so joyous that the solemnly restrained core rituals appear lifeless.

Women's central role in family religion is seen mostly in the daily observance of religious life within high-caste homes of Palashpur. Also a series of cyclical rituals called "thirteen rituals in twelve months" is performed by women, occasionally with the aid of men. Moreover, there are certain rituals where men are supported by women, for example, the "ritual of the cow shed" and the "harvest festival." Whereas the ritual of the cow shed is performed by women, men carry the freshly harvested paddy and are greeted by women in the harvest festival.

Among the daily rituals in high-caste homes, the most important is the lighting of the evening lamp by a young daughter or wife. Every Thursday, the house deity, Laxmi, is worshiped by a woman of the family. Of course, this worship is performed more elaborately as an annual event during the celebration of Laxmi-puja, discussed earlier. Moreover, women begin to observe several rituals, called *brata*, very early in life—after their initiation into *sanjpujani brata* in early years. (As we said earlier, *sanjpujani brata* is a women's ritual performed at sunset.) That is, *sanjpujani brata* initiates girls into a number of other *bratas* for women. A girl of six or older can start this *brata* by worshiping and praying to God. The *brata* rites are simple and are performed with chanting of Bengali rhymes asking for good husbands, happy homes, good in-laws, and blessings for the girl's father and for her in-law's family. Several of the chants also seem to reveal women's anxiety about the possibility of their husbands becoming attracted to or even marrying other women.

Unmarried girls observe an annual fasting and worship of Lord Siva (Sivaratri *brata*) in order to insure marrying a faithful and loving husband like Siva. Girls continue adding *bratas* throughout their lives, for example, a *brata* for their husbands' health, for children, for family, and so forth. In some of the *brata,* men join women in seeking blessing for family and children. Flowers and food are distributed ritually among adults and children, and sometimes sweets are thrown into the air for children to catch, causing great excitement among the youngsters.

Religious life of the family thus centers around women of the family, but children are regular participants in many rituals such as the ritual feast for an expectant mother. Here the expectant mother is given delicacies and new saris, but she must sit surrounded by children who share food with her. After childbirth another set of rituals is performed by women. In one, a Brahman priest officiates to name the child. Subsequently, an important event is the baby's first rice-taking ritual. Here a Brahman performs an ancestor worship for the patrilineage. However, the mother's brother feeds the rice to the baby, a familiar feature in patrilineal society to balance the asymmetry in a patriarchal social structrure. (The mother's brother's presence is also essential during a woman's wedding.)

The ritual for brothers is another important ritual in family relationships. Two days after Kalipuja (in October–November), brothers and sisters of all castes take a morning bath together, put on clean clothes, and fast until the ritual is over. Sisters collect sandalwood paste, morning dew from the grass, yogurt, and other ritual objects, and they put dots of these on their brothers' foreheads, murmuring a verse: "Yama, the immortal god of death, received this dot from his sister Yamuna. I place a dot on my brother's forehead to put thorns at the gate of Yama [meaning death]." An oil lamp is then rotated in front of the brother's face. Along with the blowing of the conch shell and ululation, the elder sibling then sprinkles *durba* grass and a little paddy on the head of the younger sibling, who bows by touching the elder's feet. After a series of such ceremonies, sisters offer food to their brothers, who in turn offer gifts to their sisters. This ritual also provides an occasion for married women to visit their parents' home. Moreover, a woman may accept any man of her brother's rank, and through an appropriate ritual establish a fictive brother-sister relationship.

Attempts to establish a spiritual bond between brothers and sisters is also demonstrated in the aforementioned *sanjpujani brata* performed by young girls. After four consecutive years of observance of this *brata*, a sister offers gifts such as an umbrella, shoes, and clothing to her brother. The brother, after a bath where he immerses his body and head in water, wears his new clothes and sits on a flat wooden seat. He holds the umbrella and rotates it while his sister showers him with different homemade sweets made of puffed rice and pressed rice. The sweets are then collected and distributed to all present. The "ritual for brothers" and the *sanjpujani brata* thus create an alliance between brothers and sisters (and cousins of the opposite sex), assuring women emotional security, help, and protection when they are needed (Chaki-Sircar 1973).

The spiritual bond between husbands and wives is also recognized in the daily act of married women putting vermillion powder in the middle of their hair, along with a vermillion dot on their forehead. These adornments are put there after women bathe, except when the women are menstruating or on other tabooed occasions such as a few days after a birth or the death of a family member. *Sindur* is not only an auspicious mark in all religious ceremonies, but it is also believed that a wife's *sindur* helps her husband's longevity and health. As we mentioned before, a married woman is thus compared with the goddess Laxmi, who brings prosperity and happiness to the home.

Family life in Palashpur is constantly stimulated by rites and festivities where women decorate the doorsteps and sometimes the courtyard with white paint made of rice powder and water. Using these traditional designs (called *alpana*), blowing conch shells, ululating, and wearing *sindur* all overlay a spiritual sentiment about women's role in the family. Girls in Palashpur, unlike boys, have the advantage of growing up with well-defined roles as mother, wife, and daughter. Women gain esteem as devoted wives, affectionate sisters, and particularly as nurturing and protective mothers. The life cycle of a woman takes her in gradual phases from beloved, dutiful daughter, to humble daughter-in-law, and ultimately to mature wife and mother—a complete woman who attains high status in old age. In the case of boys and men, except for the sacred thread (*upanayana*) rites they do not have such clear and well-defined roles.

The foregoing highlights apparent contradictions in the Palashpur sociocultural system. On the one hand, boys are pampered as the superior sex, and young men enjoy the advantage of being superior to women, who are regarded as liabilities to their parents' families. Patriarchal rites in the high-caste portion of the community exclude women entirely from core rituals, and women are treated as social inferiors in asymmetrical relationships. On the other hand, there is no role more valued in Hindu society than the role of mother. The spiritual superiority of women's roles is constantly recognized, not only in community Mother worship but also in family relationships with women as mothers, wives, daughters, and sisters. The "feminine" qualities of nurturance, affection, and devotion are sought by men to help develop their own masculinity (see Singer 1959; Erikson 1969).

Two aspects of family religion among the untouchables appear to be distinctly different from those of the high castes. Although untouchables express a deep veneration for mother deities, their family rituals express more of an egalitarian relationship between the sexes. Also, the patriarchal rituals for the lineage are not performed among them. Untouchable women wear *sindur* without recognizing the implications for the indissolubility of marriage. Among the untouchables there are no rituals for evening light, or Laxmipuja. However, in some homes untouchable women observe Manashapuja on Tuesdays, and they maintain an altar with a cactus, called Manasha. Untouchable women follow high-caste manners by using rather simple decorative designs (*alpana*), blowing conch shells, ululating and observing some high-caste *bratas* by offering gifts to the temple. As with high-caste women, untouchable women also observe the ritual of the cow shed, the harvest ritual, and the ritual for brothers. In Baen homes, brothers too reciprocate the rituals and prayers for the benefit of their sisters. This expresses the special value of women in their parents' home, a phenomenon absent in high-caste families.

In Palashpur, maleness or femaleness is not recognized as mutually exclusive. The bisexual Ardhanareesvar (the god who is man on the right half and woman on the left, a representation of Siva and his consort Parvati) symbolizes this concept. This is also followed in the religious philosophy of Vaisnavas, one school of high-caste Hindu religious philosophy. Child socialization and adult personality development in Palashpur, discussed in the following chapter, may be understood fully only in the context of this sociocultural perspective.

PART II

Maternal Acceptance and Its Correlates in Palashpur

CHAPTER 6

Socialization Research in Palashpur

Theory and Concepts

Part 2 uses the previous ethnographic portrait of Palashpur to contextualize children's and adults' perceptions of maternal acceptance-rejection in the village. Part 2 also deals with the determinants, correlates, and consequences of maternal acceptance in Palashpur.

The Warmth Dimension of Parenting

The warmth dimension of parenting (a continuum of behavior) is defined at one extreme as "parental acceptance," that is, as the love and affection parents show their children. The other end of the dimension is defined as "parental rejection," that is, as the absence or significant withdrawal of love and affection. As shown in figure 4, parental acceptance may be expressed the world over by approving of one's children, playing with them, enjoying them, fondling them, comforting and counseling them, cuddling them, praising them, singing lullabies to them, kissing, caressing, and hugging them, or demonstrating love in other actions or words. Accepting parents generally like their children, they appreciate their children's personality, and they take an

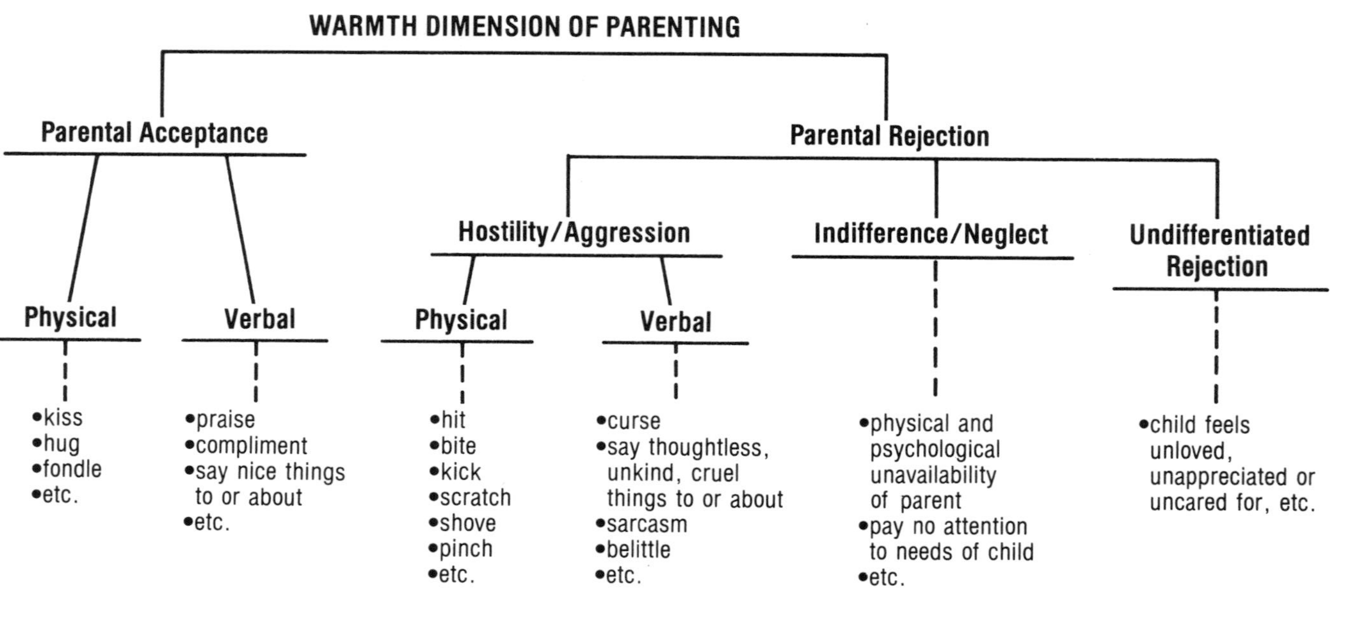

FIGURE 4. Conceptual framework of principal parenting concepts in parental acceptance-rejection theory.

interest in their children's activities and well-being. All of these things help children feel loved, wanted, and cared for.

Of course different parents display different amounts of these accepting behaviors, and some parents give their children none of them. Children raised by parents who display few or no accepting behaviors are likely to feel unloved or unwanted, that is, rejected. Rejecting parents often dislike, disapprove of, or resent their children. In many cases they view their children as a burden, and they sometimes compare their children unfavorably with other children. Around the world, parental rejection is expressed in two major forms – as hostility/aggression on the one hand and as indifference/neglect on the other (Rohner 1975, 1980, 1986). Hostility and indifference are internal, emotional states motivating many of the rejecting behaviors of parents; aggression and neglect are the observable outcomes of these motivational states. Hostile, aggressive parents may vent their anger in such physical ways as hitting, kicking, shaking, choking, burning, scratching, and shoving their children. Or these angry parents may reject their children verbally by cursing them, saying thoughtless, unkind, cruel things to or about them, being sarcastic toward them, and the like. Indifferent/neglecting parents, on the other hand, are more likely to be physically or psychologically remote or unavailable to their children. Neglecting parents often pay little attention to the physical or emotional needs and wishes of their children, and they may ignore their children's cries for attention, help, or comfort. Not infrequently these parents forget promises made to their children, and they fail to attend to other details or needs important to the children's happiness and well-being.

Parental Acceptance-Rejection Theory

Parental acceptance and rejection may be studied from two points of view, as subjectively experienced and reported by the individual or as "objectively" assessed by an outside investigator. Parental acceptance-rejection theory (Rohner 1980, 1986) assumes axiomatically that parent rejection has its most consistent and predictable effects on individuals insofar as they subjectively perceive their parents' behavior as being accepting or rejecting. This assumption that children's behavior may be more affected by the way they psychologically experience parents' behavior than by the actual behavior itself receives empirical support from Ausubel et al. (1954), Goldin (1969), Heilbrun (1973), Rabkin (1965), and others. For this reason we concentrate here primarily but not exclusively on the self-reports of acceptance-rejection made by Palashpur children and adults.

Parental acceptance-rejection theory (PAR theory, or simply PART) predicts that the perceptions of varying degrees of acceptance-rejection have consistent effects on the personality development and functioning of children and adults everywhere.[1] Research and clinical reports in the United States support this expectation in that rejection has been implicated repeatedly in a wide range of personality and behavioral disorders including various forms of mental illness, delinquency and conduct problems, poor concept formation, academic problems, and the like. (See Rohner and Nielsen 1978 for a two-volume cataloging of the consequences of parental acceptance-rejection. See also Rohner 1986.) PAR theory predicts that children everywhere who perceive themselves to be rejected tend, more than children who perceive themselves to be accepted, to report a specific constellation of personality dispositions, which include: (1) hostility, aggression, passive aggression, or problems with the management of hostility and aggression; (2) dependence or defensive independence, depending on the severity, chronicity, and form of rejection experienced; (3) impaired feelings of self-esteem, and (4) impaired feelings of self-adequacy; (5) emotional instability; (6) emotional unresponsiveness; and (7) negative worldview.

Drawing from PART we expect each of these personality dispositions to result from rejection for the following reasons. First, it seems that all of us tend to view ourselves as we imagine "significant others" view us; if we feel that our parents—as the

1. This portion of parental acceptance-rejection theory—that is, the portion dealing with the expected personality outcomes of perceived rejection—is referred to as "PART's personality theory" (Rohner 1986). Other aspects of PART such as "coping theory" (Rohner 1980, 1986)—that is, the portion of the theory that attempts to explain why some rejected children do not respond to perceived rejection as fully as most rejected children—is not treated in this book.

most significant of "others"—rejected us as children, we are likely to define ourselves as unworthy of love and therefore as unworthy and inadequate human beings. In this way we develop a sense of overall negative self-evaluation, including feelings of negative self-esteem and negative self-adequacy.

Moreover, according to PART, rejected children are likely to be more dependent—to feel clingy, possessive, and to seek parental approval, nurturance, attention, and physical contact than accepted children, because it seems, or at least acceptance-rejection theory postulates, that if children's "significant others" are rejecting, their needs for warmth and affection are unfulfilled and they will, up to a point, increase their efforts to get love and attention. In other words, they become more dependent. Beyond a certain point, according to PART, dependency responses may be extinguished or transformed. Many seriously rejected children have not learned how to give love because they have never known a loving parent after whom they can model their own behavior, and for reasons described below, even though they crave affection they have difficulty accepting it. In order to protect themselves from more emotional hurt, children who perceive themselves to be rejected tend to wrap their emotions in cotton, as it were, to encyst their emotions. Ultimately they may stop trying to get affection and other positive responses from the people who are so important to them. That is, dependency responses disappear. Thus, rejected children become emotionally insulated, unable to freely and openly form warm, lasting, intimate relations with others. Their attachments tend to be troubled by emotional constriction or defensiveness, and in extreme cases rejected children may become apathetic or emotionally bland or flat. In addition, as a result of the psychological damage brought about by perceived rejection, rejected children are inclined to have less tolerance for stress, and they are therefore likely to be less emotionally stable than those who were accepted as children.

Rejected children are apt to become resentful or angry at their parents, as well as fearful of more rejection, thereby producing what PART calls "defensive independence"—a kind of emotional withdrawal from them. In so doing, children who feel rejected initiate a process of counter-rejection. Behind this defensive independence or emotional detachment, though, is often an unrecognized longing to reestablish a warm, nurturant relationship with their parents.

Rejected children are, according to PART, especially likely to become hostile, aggressive, or passive-aggressive if rejection is seen as taking the form of parental hostility. Under these conditions, rejected children are given an aggressive model to emulate, and thus their own aggressive responses may intensify. In settings where they are not allowed to express aggression overtly, however, rejected children are likely to have problems managing their hostility. Continuously suppressed, overcontrolled aggression may be expressed in such disguised or symbolic forms as a worried preoccupation with aggression, aggressive fantasies or dreams, or in an unusual concern about the real or imagined aggression of others.

Finally, rejected children–children who are anxious, hostile, insecure, emotionally unstable, and who devaluate their feelings of self-worth and self-adequacy–are likely to generalize these feelings onto the nature of the world, experiencing it as an unfriendly, hostile, unpleasant place in which to live. Children who have experienced so much psychological hurt at the hands of their parents often come to expect little more from life itself. The very nature of life for many of them is threatening, dangerous, and unhappy. Therefore, PART postulates that these children are likely to develop a negative worldview. This process derives from the fact that the interpretations children make about the world seem to be based on their own experiences with it, both experiences they have had as individuals and experiences they know or believe others to have had. An individual's worldview extends this interpretation about the empirical world–including interpretation of the experiences a person has had at the hands of those who are most important–into an interpretation of the very *nature* of the world.

Even though they may want to reach out to others, children who perceive themselves to be rejected are often unable to form fully satisfying social relations with their peers, and so their already damaged sense of self-esteem and self-adequacy is reinforced, and they may withdraw even further into themselves. Thus as predicted in PART, in the absence of positive, counteracting experiences over time (such as rewarding peer relations), these rejected children are likely to mature into adults who are hostile (or have trouble managing their anger), insecure, and somewhat dependent (or defensively independent), who have feelings of impaired self-esteem and impaired self-adequacy, who have a negative worldview, and who are somewhat emotionally unstable. Moreover, PAR theory states that many adults who felt rejected as children tend to have strong needs for affection, but they are often unable to return it because they have been more or less emotionally insulated or unresponsive to potentially close interpersonal relations. Any of these adults who become parents are expected by PART to be more likely to reject their own children than parents who felt accepted as children. In this way the rejection cycle is perpetuated, and along with it the personality constellation just described.

To summarize briefly, a central postulate of parental acceptance-rejection theory is that each of the seven personality dispositions described above is likely to appear to a significantly greater degree among children who perceive themselves to be rejected than among children who perceive themselves to be accepted. These outcomes of perceived rejection versus acceptance are expected to appear the world over, regardless of variations in culture, language, race, geographic region, or other limiting condition. Similarly, the theory postulates that adults everywhere who report having been rejected as children are likely to experience these personality dispositions to a greater degree than adults who report having been accepted as children.

Hostility, dependency (or defensive independence), negative self-esteem, negative self-adequacy, emotional instability, emotional unresponsiveness, and negative worldview do not exhaust the expected effects of parental rejection. Indeed, we earlier listed other consequences of parental rejection observed at least in the United States, and it seems likely that parental rejection may lurk behind many other behavioral and psychological disorders of both children and adults. In fact, Rohner (1975, 1986) has shown that the antecedents and consequences of parental rejection-acceptance permeate the entire fabric of life within a sociocultural system. The effects of rejection are not limited simply to individual personality and behavior disorders, but reach into such abstract domains as the religious beliefs of a people, their art, music, and other expressive behaviors. In America (Potvin 1977) as well as cross-culturally (Rohner 1975), for example, it has been reported that rejected children tend to view God, the gods, or whatever form the supernatural takes, as being somewhat hostile, punitive, or capable of inflicting death, sickness, or misfortune. Children raised with love, on the other hand, tend to view the supernatural as warmer, kinder, and more supportive in human life.

The next chapter deals with the experiences of acceptance and rejection reported by children and their mothers in Palashpur. More specifically, the chapter examines the level of perceived maternal affection, aggression, neglect, and undifferentiated rejection reported by children and adults there. (Undifferentiated rejection refers to conditions where children feel unloved, uncared for, or unwanted without objective indications of parental hostility/aggression or indifference/neglect.) The chapter also focuses on the seven personality dispositions associated theoretically with varying degrees of acceptance and rejection, and it explores some of the significant antecedent (i.e., "causes") as well as general correlates of perceived acceptance-rejection within the sociocultural context of village life. Before going to those topics, however, we outline below major features of the research design employed in the "socialization research" component of this study.

Design of Socialization Research in Palashpur

Sample

Information in the next chapter is based on an intracommunity sample of fifty-two families with children between the ages of six through twelve years. To the extent possible, these children—twenty-three males and twenty-nine females—were drawn in a stratified random sample from all caste levels within the village. Twenty-seven children were taken from high-caste families, and twenty-five were from untouchable families. Only one child was drawn from each household. Thus the sample comprises about

38 percent of all households within the village (the village comprises 138 households, with 1,275 residents), but it represents the majority of households with children between the ages of six through twelve.

A highly generalized profile of the average family in the sample includes a thirty-nine-year-old father and a thirty-six-year-old mother with four children. If they are of an untouchable caste, these people are likely to live in a nuclear family household with mother, father, and their children only; if they are members of one of the high castes, these people may live in either a nuclear family household or in some form of extended family household with the children's paternal grandparents. (Unlike other high-caste families in the sample, Brahmans are likely to live in some form of extended family household that includes the children's paternal grandparents, but only two Brahman families in the sample live in the classic joint family household.) In the typical untouchable home approximately six people (parents and four children) live together, whereas eight people reside in the average high-caste home comprising one or both paternal grandparents, parents, children, and sometimes the father's sibling(s).

The majority of untouchable mothers in the sample are illiterate, whereas the average high-caste mother has completed one of the first three grades in school. All untouchable fathers in the sample are illiterate, but the average high-caste father has graduated from at least the ninth grade. The typical child in the sample is a middle-born nine-year-old.

Research Design and Instruments

As shown in greater detail in table 2, the research design in the socialization component of this work called for (*a*) systematic time-sampled behavior observations of the interaction between parents and children within sample households, and of children's behavior in public settings; (*b*) formal interviews with parents and sample children; and (*c*) the administration of a battery of self-report questionnaires (in Bengali) about children's and parents' (mothers' and fathers') perceptions of parental acceptance-rejection and the relevant personality dispositions

TABLE 2 Instruments and Procedures Used in the Study of Parental Acceptance and Rejection in Palashpur

INSTRUMENT/PROCEDURE	USED AS A MEASURE OF
Self-report questionaires	
Mother (Father) PARQ	Mother's (or father's) perception of her/his behavior toward her/his child in terms of acceptance-rejection.
Child PARQ	Child's perception of parent's acceptance-rejection.
Adult PARQ	Adult's perception of treatment received by own parents in terms of acceptance-rejection.
Mother PAQ	Adult's (usually mother's) assessment of the behavioral dispositions of the child (seven dispostions measured).
Child PAQ	Child's self-reported personality and behavioral dispositions (seven dispositions measured).
Adult PAQ	Adult's self-reported personality and behavioral dispositions (seven dispositions reported.)
Interviews	
Parental Acceptance-Rejection Interview Schedule (PARIS), Adult version	Determination of child's major caretaker(s) and alternate caretaker(s); parent's (usually mother's) evaluation of parents' (mother's and father's) behavior in terms of acceptance-rejection and permissiveness-strictness; parent's perception of (*a*) availability of one or more "nurturant others" for child, and (*b*) the extent to which the child is in social isolation or interaction with others.
Child PARIS	Child's perception of parental (mother's and father's) acceptance-rejection behavior; perception of parental (mother's and father's) control; perception of own abil-

TABLE 2 *(continued)*

INSTRUMENT/PROCEDURE	USED AS A MEASURE OF
	ity to cope with perceived acceptance-rejection and control.
Behavior observations	Direct observation of interaction between parent and child (in terms of acceptance-rejection and child's behavioral dispositions), and of interaction between child and peers (in terms of seven behavioral dispositions).
Background data schedule	Social-situational and demographic information about the family.

described earlier.[2] A member of the research team read aloud the questionnaires, item by item, to illiterate respondents. All other respondents read the questionnaires themselves. All questionnaires were administered within the village on an individual basis.

In addition to responding to these questionnaires, interviews, and behavior observation procedures, sample mothers responded to a background data schedule that elicited detailed demographic and social-situational information about each family. Complete details about the procedures and instruments used in the research are provided in the *Handbook for the Study of Parental Acceptance and Rejection* (Rohner 1984).

The Self-report Questionnaires

Because of PAR theory's emphasis on the phenomenological or self-report perspective described above (and in Rohner 1986), the

2. The English-language version of the self-report questionnaires was translated into Bengali and then translated back into English by separate bilingual translators. The two English-language versions of the questionnaire were compared and faulty translations were corrected—in a process of translation/back translation—until a satisfactory Bengali version of each instrument was created.

remainder of this book concentrates on an analysis of self-report questionnaire data regarding maternal acceptance-rejection and personality. The next chapter also incorporates information from the background data questionnaire. Subsequent writings will report on results from behavior observations and interviews and will compare results across the various measurement modalities. The self-report questionnaires are described at greater length below, as an aide to interpreting results in chapter 7.

PARENTAL ACCEPTANCE-REJECTION QUESTIONNAIRE. The Parental Acceptance-Rejection Questionnaire (PARQ) measures respondents' assessments of their (or their children's) childhood experiences in terms of perceived parental warmth (i.e., acceptance-rejection). Three versions of the PARQ were used (Rohner 1984): (1) The Mother PARQ asks parents (usually mothers but sometimes other major caretakers such as fathers) to respond according to their perceptions about the way they treat their own children. (2) The Adult PARQ asks mothers and fathers to reflect on the way they were each treated when they were children between seven and twelve years of age. (3) The Child PARQ asks children between six and twelve years of age to reflect on the way their primary caretaker (usually the mother) now treats them. In all three versions, respondents assess parental behavior in terms of four scales: (*a*) perceived warmth and affection, (*b*) perceived hostility and aggression, (*c*) perceived indifference and neglect, and (*d*) perceived undifferentiated rejection. (As indicated earlier, undifferentiated rejection refers to conditions where parents are perceived as withdrawing love from a child—that is, the child interprets the parent's behavior as rejecting—but where such rejection does not clearly reflect either perceived or objectively measured hostility, neglect, or indifference.) Examples of scale items on the Child PARQ are: "My mother makes me feel wanted and needed" (perceived warmth/affection); "My mother goes out of her way to hurt my feelings" (perceived hostility); "My mother ignores me as long as I do nothing to bother her" (perceived indifference/neglect); "My mother does not really love me" (perceived undifferentiated rejection). Children respond to statements such as these on a four-point, Likert-like scale ranging from "almost always true" to "almost never true."

An analysis of the validity and the reliability of the various Bengali-language versions of the PARQ, detailed in the appendix, shows the instrument to be psychometrically adequate. (For details of a comparative analysis of the English-language versions of the validity and reliability of the PARQ, see Rohner 1984.)

PERSONALITY ASSESSMENT QUESTIONNAIRE. The second self-report questionnaire, the Personality Assessment Questionnaire (PAQ), complements the PARQ and assesses respondents' perceptions of themselves with respect to the seven personality and behavioral dispositions described earlier and defined more fully below. Three versions of the PAQ were used (Rohner 1984): (1) The Mother PAQ asks parents (usually mothers) to respond according to their perceptions about their child's behavior in terms of the seven behavioral and personality dispositions listed above. (2) The Adult PAQ asks adults (mothers and fathers respectively) to reflect on their perceptions of themselves with respect to the same seven behavioral dispositions. (3) The Child PAQ asks children between six and twelve years of age to reflect on themselves with respect to the same seven behavioral dispositions. Representative items in the Adult PAQ include: "I have trouble controlling my temper" (hostility/aggression); "I like my friends to make a fuss over me when I am hurt or sick" (dependence); "I wish I could have more respect for myself" (negative self-esteem); "I feel inept in many of the things I try to do" (negative self-adequacy); "I feel distant and detached from most people" (emotional unresponsiveness); "Small setbacks upset me a lot" (emotional instability); and "I view the universe as a threatening, dangerous place" (negative wordview). As with the PARQ, children respond to statements such as these on a four-point, Likert-like scale ranging from "almost always true" to "almost never true." Analysis of the validity and reliability of the various Bengali-language versions of the PAQ, detailed in the appendix, shows the instrument to be reasonably sound, psychometrically. (Details of an analysis of validity and reliability of the English-language versions of the PAQ are provided in Rohner 1984).

Personality Concepts Defined

It is important to understand what is meant and *not* meant by each of the personality dispositions described in PART's personality theory. With this thought in mind we now give a brief description of each disposition as it is construed in PAR theory.

Hostility/Aggression

Hostility is an internal emotional reaction of anger, enmity, or resentment directed toward another person or situation or toward oneself; aggression, on the other hand, is any act that intends to hurt physically or psychologically someone (including oneself) or something. Active aggression may be manifested verbally or physically, such as cursing someone or hitting them, respectively. Passive aggression is a less direct expression of aggression, manifested in such forms as pouting, sulking, passive obstructionism, bitterness, vindictiveness, or irritability. Aggression is here distinguished conceptually from assertiveness. Assertiveness refers to individuals' attempts to thrust themselves or their ideas forward boldly or with confidence, or to place themselves in physical, verbal, social, or some other equality and/or priority over others. Unlike aggression, however, assertiveness does not imply an intention of "hurting" someone or something.

Dependence

Dependence is the *emotional* reliance of one person on another for comfort, approval, guidance, support, reassurance, and the like. Independence is the essential freedom from such emotional reliance, or at least the freedom from having to make these bids very often. The goal of dependency behavior among children is usually the elicitation of warm, effectionate attention from an adult. Indicators of dependency include clinging to the parent, attention seeking, becoming anxious, insecure, unhappy when they are separated from their parent, and so forth. As used in PART, independence is distinguished conceptually from self-reliance, which is a kind of instrumental (versus emotional) independence. That is, self-reliance refers to task-oriented behaviors, as when children seek out someone to help them untie a knot. Insofar as this act is purely a request for help with a task, the behavior pertains to self-reliance, but when it is an attempt to get attention or comfort it becomes dependence. The distinction between the two is sometimes subtle.

Self-esteem

Self-esteem is a global, emotional evaluation of oneself in terms of worth. Positive feelings of self-esteem imply that individuals like or approve of themselves, accept themselves, are comfortable with themselves, are rarely disappointed with themselves, and perceive themselves as persons of worth or worthy of respect.

Self-adequacy

Self-adequacy is an overall self-evaluation of one's competence to perform daily tasks adequately, to cope satisfactorily with daily problems, and to satisfy one's own needs. Positive feelings of self-adequacy imply that individuals view themselves as competent, able to deal satisfactorily with daily problems, and successful or capable of success in the things they set out to do.

Emotional Responsiveness

Emotional responsiveness refers to an individual's ability to express emotions freely and openly. Emotional responsiveness is revealed by the spontaneity and ease with which individuals are able to respond emotionally to other persons. Emotionally responsive people generally have little difficulty forming warm and lasting attachments, and their attachments are not troubled by emotional constriction or defensiveness. They are able to show spontaneous affection toward their friends and family, and they are able to express easily their sympathy and other feelings on appropriate occasions. Interpersonal relations of emotionally responsive people are often close and personal.

Emotional Stablity

Emotional stability refers to an individual's constancy or steadiness of mood and to the ability to withstand minor setbacks, failures, difficulties, or other stresses without becoming emotionally upset. Emotionally stable people are able to maintain their composure under minor emotional stress. They are not easily or quickly excited or angered, and they are fairly constant in their basic mood.

Worldview

Worldview is a person's often unverbalized global or overall evaluation of life and the universe as being basically a good, secure, friendly, happy, unthreatening place (positive worldview) or as being a bad, insecure, threatening, unpleasant, hostile, or uncertain place (negative worldview). Worldview does not refer to an individuals' empirically derived knowledge of the economic, political, social, or natural environment.

CHAPTER 7

Maternal Acceptance and Its Effects and Determinants in Palashpur

The five major sections of this chapter deal with several interrelated issues. In the first we attempt briefly to localize maternal behavior in Palashpur (particularly the warmth dimension of parenting there) within the broad sociocultural context of India itself. Here we develop a profile of perceived maternal acceptance experienced by children as well as by adults in their own childhoods for three regions of India. We concentrate more on *mothers'* acceptance-rejection than on the relative level of acceptance of any other caretaker because, as noted in chapter 4, mothers in India are most commonly the major caretakers of young children—though grandmothers, older siblings, fathers, and others often assume this responsibility. Moreover, in this and the other sections we concentrate on overall acceptance-rejection as well as on maternal warmth and affection per se, as measured by the PARQ.

The second section of chapter 7 provides a brief descriptive profile of the two children in Palashpur who perceive themselves to be truly rejected; the third section reviews the psychosocial effects of varying degrees of perceived maternal acceptance-rejection among children and among Palashpur adults (especially mothers) in their childhoods. This section also reviews evidence bearing on the major postulates of PART's personality theory described in the preceding chapter. In the course of describing evidence pertinent to PART's personality theory we develop a profile of children's and mothers' typical personality dispositions and relative levels of psychosocial functioning within the village. In the fourth section, we explore some of the significant determinants of variations in perceived maternal acceptance-rejection in Palashpur. Especially important here are caste, gender, and age. Finally, the last section reviews and summarizes major conclusions drawn earlier about significant effects and determinants of perceived maternal acceptance in Palashpur.

Comparative Perspective on Maternal Warmth within India

Numerous anthropological studies throughout the Indian subcontinent report that Indian mothers display relatively little overt warmth. More specifically, Minturn and Hitchcock (1966), for example, found that among the Rajputs (a caste group) in the village of Khalapur, infants were seldom given special attention beyond their physical needs. In fact they wrote, "adults are not overly affectionate with children of any age" (p. 137). When Minturn and Lambert (1964) compared the results of the Khalapur study with data collected using the same interview procedures in the other five communities of the Whitings' (Whiting 1963) Six Cultures Project (namely in the United States, Mexico, Kenya, Okinawa, and the Philippines), they concluded that "Khalapur mothers are unusual in their lack of warmth in interaction with their children" (1964, 238). They found the Rajputs there to be considerably below the pancultural mean in terms of maternal warmth, and they described these people as notably unresponsive to the needs of their children (1964, 230).

It is risky to generalize about Indian parents from a study of a single caste within a single Indian community (cf. Lannoy 1971). However, additional evidence supports the claim that, regardless of caste or class affiliation, parent-child relations in India seem not to be significantly warm or affectionate, at least with regard to nontribal groups. For example, in a sample of 101 societies

(Rohner 1975), three out of the four Indian communities represented in the world sample scored below the worldwide mean of parental warmth and affection. Note that in this study a variety of caste/class groups were represented in the three Indian communities classified in the holocultural study as rejecting. The one Indian group characterized as having a high level of warmth in parent-child relations was in fact a tribal group (the Murias)—a group only partly assimilated into the larger Hindu society.

Furthermore, in an observational study of various caste/class groups in the city of Bhubaneswar, the capital of Orissa, Seymour (1976) reported that "there were certain general patterns of child care which characterized all [caste/class] categories of household" (p. 787). Summarizing these patterns, Seymour pointed out that "first of all, the presence of children, although highy desired, was taken for granted, and a new baby was generally treated as simply one more member of the household, not the center of attention. His physical needs were attended to, but otherwise the child received little in the way of focused attention and stimulation. In fact, there was a prohibition on praising children and otherwise calling special attention to them" (pp. 787–88). Seymour also found from her behavior observations in Bhubaneswar that mothers and their surrogates "were not highly responsive to their children's requests" and that "the child was rarely treated as an individual with special attention given to his particular feelings and needs" (p. 788). Observations such as these, in conjunction with her own comparative review of parent-child relations in India, ultimately led Seymour to conclude that "cross-cultural literature suggests that low maternal warmth is a salient factor in Indian households" (1983, 266–67).

While this conclusion about low maternal warmth in Indian households is highly suggestive, none of these studies examined the warmth dimension of parenting in any great detail, at least not as construed in parental acceptance-rejection theory. When that is done, especially when maternal acceptance-rejection is studied from the *children's* own point of view as we do here, it becomes apparent that conclusions about low maternal warmth in Indian families require significant revision—at least for Palashpur and the other parts of India discussed below.

TABLE 3 Perceived Maternal Acceptance-Rejection (PARQ) in Three States of India

STATE	LANGUAGE	CHILD PARQ				ADULT PARQ			
		M	S.D.	*N*	Ave. Age	*M*	S.D.	*N*	Ave. Age
Andra Pradesh	Telugu	126.2	23.94	107	11.5	111.7	28.20	99	28.8
Madhya Pradesh	Hindi	102.8	22.68	70	10.0	100.4	24.90	40	unknown
West Bengal	Bengali	109.8	14.82	50	9.2	96.4	16.73	51	23.0

Note: Data in table are drawn from Rohner 1986. Data from Andra Pradesh were reported by N. Y. Reddy; data for Madhya Pradesh were reported by Jai Prakash; data for West Bengal were reported by Manjusri Chaki-Sircar.

Maternal Warmth in Palashpur Compared with Other Regions of India

India appears to be a land of significant contrasts in perceived maternal acceptance-rejection, as shown in table 3. The Child PARQ and the Adult PARQ were administered in three widely dispersed locations within India and in three different languages (namely, Telugu, Hindi, and Bengali) to children and adults respectively. Telugu-speaking children in village and urban settings around the south Indian city of Hyderabad scored quite high (M = 126.2) on the Child PARQ.[1] Indeed, 14 percent of them scored at or above 150 on the Child PARQ, indicating the feeling of being more rejected than accepted. These results support conclusions drawn by researchers who report low maternal warmth in their respective field sites. Reflecting on their childhood, Telugu-speaking adults in the same locations, on the other hand, scored on the average much lower on the PARQ than did the children (M = 111.7). Nonetheless, 10 percent of them also reported that they were rejected as children.

Both Hindi-speaking children and adults in and around the town of Saugar in central India's Madhya Pradesh scored fairly low on the PARQ, indicating the perception of considerable maternal warmth and affection, low maternal hostility and aggression, low maternal indifference and neglect, low maternal undifferentiated rejection, and low overall rejection (Child PARQ, M = 102.8; Adult PARQ, M = 100.4). According to Jai Prakash (pers. comm. August 1980) only about 4 percent of these Hindi-speaking children reported themselves as rejected by their mothers. The number of children who perceive themselves as rejected (i.e., with a Child PARQ score at or above 150) in the east Indian village of Palashpur is even smaller. There, only about 2 percent of the children experience maternal rejection to a significant degree. As shown in table 3, children's mean PARQ score there is 109.8; the mean PARQ score for adults in Palashpur is even lower, at 96.4 (Adult PARQ, father version, M = 96.35; Adult PARQ, mother version, M = 96.72).

We have no satisfactory explanation at this time for these significant regional differences in perceived acceptance-rejection.

1. M refers to the mean or arithmetic average.

Of course in each of these three locations there is a substantial range of variation in the perception of acceptance-rejection, but overall, data from Madhya Pradesh and West Bengal suggest that any generalized conclusion regarding low warmth in Indian families requires significant revision, at least when viewed through the eyes of Indian adults and children themselves. This revised perspective on Indian parenting is in keeping with Kakar's (1978) generalized observations, which emphasize substantial maternal warmth in Indian families, especially for very young children.

Maternal Acceptance-Rejection in Palashpur

As we said earlier, both children and adults in Palashpur experience on the average—but with at least a few notable exceptions (two of which are discussed later)—considerable maternal acceptance. Table A.1 in the appendix documents this conclusion in detail for children and for mothers recalling their own childhood. From that table one can see that children and adults in Palashpur tend to report high levels of maternal warmth and affection, occasional hostility and aggression, fairly low levels of indifference and neglect, and at least occasional undifferentiated rejection. For every form of perceived acceptance, the mothers' Adult PARQ scores are slightly lower than children's PARQ scores, indicating an overall tendency for the women to perceive their own childhoods slightly but significantly more favorably than children perceive theirs (Adult PARQ, mother version, $M = 96.35$; Child PARQ, $M = 109.82$, $t = 4.22$, $p < .001$).[2] It is unclear why mothers' childhoods are characterized by greater perceived acceptance than today's children experience, though some of the discrepancy in reported warmth scores (i.e., total PARQ scores) might reflect a tendency for mothers to idealize their childhoods.

It also appears from table A.1—for currently unexplained reasons—that mothers report their own childhood to have been characterized by modestly but significantly greater ($t = 3.91$,

2. t refers to the t-test statistic; p refers to the probability value of the statistical test, in this case to the t-test.

$p < .001$) maternal acceptance (Adult PARQ, mother version, $M = 96.35$) than they report giving to their children today (Mother PARQ, $M = 107.76$). Nonetheless, children agree with their mothers' reports that, on the average, children in Palashpur experience substantially more acceptance than rejection, as revealed by total scores on both the Mother PARQ ($M = 107.76$) and the Child PARQ ($M = 109.82$). (The difference between these two PARQ scores is not statistically significant: $t = .76$, $p =$ n.s.).[3]

Rejected Children of Palashpur: Two Case Studies

Even though the great majority of children in Palashpur experience substantial maternal acceptance, one child reports having been seriously rejected by her mother (where, as indicated earlier, maternal rejection is revealed in the PARQ by scores at or above 150 points). A second child approaches closely the criterion (with a PARQ score of 144); for that reason, she is included in the following abbreviated portraits of rejected children in Palashpur.

Champa Bala

Champa, an eight-year-old girl in a Kayastha (high-caste) nuclear family, perceives herself to be more rejected by her mother—her major caretaker—than does any other child in Palashpur. More specifically, she perceives her mother to be cold and unaffectionate (low warmth scale = 57), somewhat hostile and aggressive (hostility scale = 40), quite indifferent and neglecting (indifference scale = 49), and somewhat undifferentiated rejecting (rejection scale = 30). Overall her total PARQ score of 176 places her well above the test's midpoint of 150 where children experience themselves qualitatively to be more rejected than accepted.

In addition to experiencing significant maternal rejection, Champa lives in a household characterized by her mother as one of serious conflict between herself and her husband. Moreover,

3. Correlations between individual Mother PARQ scales and Child PARQ scales, as well as between the total Mother PARQ and Child PARQ, are reported in the appendix.

her mother (on the Mother PARQ) admits to being fairly cold toward Champa (low warmth scale = 50), sometimes hostile and aggressive (hostile scale = 29), sometimes indifferent and neglecting (indifference scale = 30), and often undifferentiated rejecting (rejection scale = 22). Her overall Mother PARQ score (total PARQ = 132), however, does not reach the point where she acknowledges greater rejection than acceptance of the girl. Nonetheless, it is one of the two highest Mother PARQ scores in the village. (It is unclear to what extent Champa's father or other caretakers might also reject her or possibly provide some warmth and support for the girl.)

As one expects from parental acceptance-rejection theory, Champa's mental health is negatively affected by this rejection and parental conflict (Child PAQ score = 102). More specifically, she suffers from impaired feelings of self-esteem (PAQ scale = 16) and impaired feelings of self-adequacy (PAQ scale = 16); she is extremely dependent (PAQ scale = 24); she reports herself to be a little emotionally unresponsive (PAQ scale = 12) and emotionally unstable (PAQ scale = 12); she has slight problems with hostility/aggression (PAQ scale = 11), and she has a slightly negative worldview (PAQ scale = 11). Overall, Champa's mother concurs strikingly with her daughter's self-appraisals (as measured by the Mother PAQ = 100), but she regards her daughter as being even less emotionally responsive (Mother PAQ scale = 19) than the girl perceives herself to be.

Manica Rani

Manica, the second-most rejected child in the village, is the nine-year-old daughter in a Brahman family of eight. She sees her mother, who is also her major caretaker, as often being reasonably warm (low warmth scale = 39), but at the same time often slightly rejecting in the sense of being somewhat hostile and aggressive (hostility scale = 39), indifferent and neglecting (indifference scale = 39), and undifferentiated rejecting (rejection scale = 27). Overall Manica's PARQ score reaches 144, a score just below the midpoint of 150. In an interview with the girl, Manica reported that both her mother and her father sometimes slap her, yell at her, scold her, and send her away to another room when she displeases them. But both parents also sometimes hug and kiss her, and they occasionally praise her when she does well.

Manica's mother agreed with this appraisal of her own behavior and of her husband's behavior toward the girl. Moreover, her Mother PARQ scores—which were among the highest in the village (Mother PARQ = 134)—tended to agree fairly closely with Manica's scores. Indeed, Manica's mother reported the identical level of maternal hostility and aggression (hostility scale = 39) toward the girl, and only slightly different undifferentiated rejection (rejection scale = 29). However, she reported herself to be somewhat warmer (low warmth scale = 33) and less indifferent (indifferent scale = 33) than Manica saw her as being. Behavior observations of the interaction between Manica and her mother showed that Manica's mother is sometimes sarcastic and curt with her daughter, and she sometimes threatens to tell the girl's older brothers (of whom Manica is afraid) or her father about her misbehavior. According to the threat, one of these men will then beat her. Manica's mother also expresses her displeasure by threatening to deprive the girl of food. Manica often feels that she does not deserve this treatment from her mother.

In addition to spending a considerable amount of time with her sometimes-rejecting mother, Manica spends considerable time with her paternal grandmother, with whom she feels close and who often defends her when her mother becomes too punitive. Manica also feels close to her paternal aunt who lives next door. The presence of both of these alternate caretakers seems to help cushion the hurt of her mother's episodic rejection.

Overall the level of Manica's social-emotional functioning (as assessed by the Child PAQ) is fairly positive. As expected in parental acceptance-rejection theory discussed more fully later, however, she reports herself as having some problems with the management of hostility and aggression (PAQ scale = 14), she is somewhat unresponsive emotionally (PAQ scale = 16), and she is quite dependent (PAQ scale = 17). But she feels fairly good about herself in terms of self-esteem (PAQ scale = 10) and self-adequacy (PAQ scale = 11); she is fairly stable emotionally (PAQ scale = 12); and she has a very positive worldview (PAQ scale = 8). On the Mother PAQ, Manica's mother tends clearly to concur

TABLE 4 Correlations between Perceived Rejection (Total PARQ) and Personality Dispositions (PAQ Scales) among Adults (Mothers) and Children in Palashpur

	PERSONALITY DISPOSITIONS							
RESPONDENT	Aggression	Dependence	Negative Self-esteem	Negative Self-adequacy	Emotional Unresponsiveness	Emotional Instability	Negative Worldview	Overall PAQ Score
Adult (*N* = 47)	.57***	-.10	.29*	.37***	.51***	.52***	.71***	.64***
Child (*N* = 50)	.17	-.11	.15	.35**	.43**	-.16	.23*	.29*

$^{*}p < .05$.
$^{**}p < .01$.
$^{***}p < .001$.

with the child's self-assessment (Mother PAQ = 89; Child PAQ = 88). No doubt the availability of the warm, supportive alternate caretakers helps Manica cope with perceived maternal rejection (Rohner 1986).

Effects of Perceived Acceptance-Rejection in Palashpur

As the preceding vignettes suggest, an individual's perceptions of parental acceptance-rejection affect his or her level of social-emotional functioning. This is true for both adults and children in Palashpur, as shown in table 4. There one sees that the degree to which Palashpur mothers report themselves as having positive feelings of self-esteem and self-adequacy, as being emotionally responsive and emotionally stable, as having a positive worldview, as having few problems with hostility and aggression, and as having overall positive mental health (as assessed by the total PAQ) is related directly to the degree of maternal acceptance they experienced in their own childhoods.[4]

The mothers' level of dependence failed to relate as predicted by PAR theory to perceived maternal acceptance. This failure of dependence to relate significantly to perceived acceptance-rejection—for both mothers and their children—is probably due more to PARQ's incomplete assessment of the "dependency" construct (see Rohner 1986) than to a true lack of relationship between the two variables.

Table 4 also shows that the relationship between personality and perceived acceptance-rejection among children in Palashpur is apparently weaker than the same relationship among mothers. That is, only three personality dispositions (namely, self-adequacy, emotional responsiveness, and worldview) and overall mental health (i.e., total PAQ) among children correlate significantly with perceived acceptance-rejection. The fact that aggression, self-esteem, and emotional stability do not correlate as

4. Fathers are omitted from this discussion because of the severely attenuated sample size of men ($N = 18$) who participated in this portion of the research and because of the suggestion of bias in the self-reports of those men who did participate.

predicted may be due to troublesome psychometric characteristics of the Bengali-language version of the Child PAQ described in the appendix. Indeed, the overall lowering of children's correlations in relation to mothers' correlations in table 4 is mathematically expectable given the weaker psychometric characteristics of the Bengali-language version of the Child PAQ in relation to the Bengali-language version of the Adult PAQ (mother version). Nonetheless it is important to note that children's overall mental health status *is* positively and significantly ($r = .29$, $p < .05$) related to perceived acceptance in Palashpur.[5] This conclusion is enhanced by the fact that the correlation between the Mother PARQ (i.e., mothers' self-reports of their maternal acceptance) and the Child PAQ (i.e., children's self-assessment of their personality functioning) ($r = .27$, $p = .057$) is nearly identical with the correlation between the Child PARQ (i.e., childrens' perceptions of maternal acceptance) and the Child PAQ reported above.

Determinants of Perceived Maternal Warmth in Palashpur

Communities everywhere are characterized by a range of variation in perceived acceptance-rejection. Palashpur is no exception. As determined by the Child PARQ, for example, maternal warmth there ranges from quite high perceived acceptance (the lowest Child PARQ score being 92) to serious rejection (the highest Child PARQ score being 176). Several different classes of factors appear to be significant determinants of this variation in the perception of mothers' accepting or rejecting behaviors. Among the most salient determinants of variations in perceived maternal acceptance in Palashpur are, very importantly—as we said earlier—caste and gender; children's age and mothers' age are important as well. In this section we review evidence bearing on these determinants of differences in perceived acceptance. We also provide evidence suggesting several discernible factors that

5. r is the conventional statistical symbol used to designate a correlation coefficient.

help explain why caste and gender are effective predictors of variations in perceived acceptance-rejection.

Caste Differences in Perceived Maternal Acceptance

Caste affiliation in Palashpur is a major predictor of variations in perceived maternal acceptance, especially in the warmth aspect of acceptance. More specifically, perceived maternal warmth varies inversely with children's caste status: the higher the caste ranking of a family (see caste ranking in table 1), the less the maternal warmth reported by both children ($r = -.26$, $p < .08$) and their mothers ($r = -.47$, $p = .001$). Similarly, the higher the caste of a family, the more indifference/neglect children report ($r = .29$, $p < .05$) and the less overall maternal acceptance mothers report (Mother PARQ: $r = -.34$, $p < .02$). Interestingly, when mothers report on their own childhood (using the Adult PARQ, mother version) these relationships reverse. That is, the higher the mother's caste, the less indifference/neglect ($r = -.40$, $p = .004$) and the more overall acceptance she reports having experienced in her own childhood ($r = .31$, $p = .03$). Currently we have no explanation for this generational shift in caste-based perceptions of maternal acceptance.

These correlational data mask the fact that major caste distinctions in maternal behavior lie in the contrast between the four untouchable castes on the one hand and the eleven high castes on the other. A much clearer picture of caste differences in perceived maternal acceptance emerges when one examines this contrast, as shown in table 5. There one sees that both children ($t = 2.81$, $p = .007$) and their mothers ($t = 4.45$, $p = .0001$) report that high-caste children receive less maternal warmth than do untouchable children; both children and mothers also agree that high-caste children experience slightly less overall maternal acceptance (Child PARQ: $t = 2.24$, $p = .03$; Mother PARQ: $t = 2.02$, $p = .049$) than do untouchable children. Moreover, high-caste children perceive slightly more maternal indifference and neglect than do untouchable children ($t = 2.69$, $p = .01$). In her research based on behavior observations of one- through ten-year-olds and their major caretakers in the city of Bhubaneswar

TABLE 5 Caste Differences in Children's and Mothers' Perceptions of Maternal Acceptance within Palashpur

PARQ	HIGH CASTES		UNTOUCHABLES			
VERSION	*M*	S.D.	*M*	S.D.	*t*	*p*
Child PARQ						
Low warmth	31.96	9.42	25.86	5.61	2.81	.007
Host./agg.	31.04	5.72	32.05	5.73	-.61	n.s.
Indf./negl.	28.89	6.35	25.36	2.22	2.69	.01
rej. (undif.)	21.56	4.34	21.23	2.88	.32	n.s.
Ch. PARQ	113.44	17.63	104.77	8.70	2.24	.03
Mother PARQ						
Low warmth	30.22	6.30	24.09	3.07	4.45	.0001
Host./agg.	30.89	4.79	31.14	5.22	-.17	n.s.
Indif./negl.	26.00	4.40	24.91	3.27	.99	n.s.
Rej. (undif.)	23.44	3.12	23.86	2.25	-.55	n.s.
Mo. PARQ	110.52	12.81	104.00	9.74	2.02	.049
Adult PARQ (mother version)						
Low warmth	25.21	5.16	26.95	4.35	-1.29	n.s.
Host./agg.	24.07	7.91	29.27	7.18	-2.43	.02
Indif./negl.	22.50	2.59	25.50	3.26	-3.53	.001
Rej. (undif.)	18.89	4.35	21.00	3.10	-2.00	.051
Ad. PARQ	90.68	16.12	102.73	15.17	-2.71	.009

Notes: High-caste Child PARQ and Mother PARQ data are based on $N = 27$; untouchable Child PARQ and Mother PARQ data are based on $N = 22$; high-caste Adult PARQ data are based on $N = 28$; untouchable Adult PARQ data are based on $N = 22$.

(in east-central India), Seymour (1983) found the same trend: untouchable and lower-class mothers showed greater positive affect toward their children than did high-caste and higher-class mothers ($F = 44.05$, $p < .001$).[6]

These trends are reversed in Palashpur when mothers reflect on their own childhood (as reported on the Adult PARQ, mother version). There, untouchable mothers report having experienced

6. *F* designates the F-test statistic in the analysis of variance.

as children slightly more hostility/aggression ($t = -2.43$, $p = .02$), indifference/neglect ($t = -3.53$, $p = .001$), undifferentiated rejection ($t = -2.00$, $p = .051$), and less overall acceptance (Adult PARQ: $t = -2.71$, $p = .009$) than did high-caste mothers. Only with respect to perceived maternal warmth did women in the two-caste strata not experience significantly different parenting ($t = -1.29$, $p =$ n.s.) in their own childhoods. One should remember that for most villagers these caste differences tend to reflect variations with the "acceptance"–very little within the "rejection"–range of the acceptance-rejection continuum.

We have no ready explanation for caste differences between the experiences of today's children and the childhood experiences of their mothers. But several classes of factors seem to explain why high-caste mothers in Palashpur today are seen by their children and sometimes by themselves to be somewhat less accepting than untouchable mothers. The most important of these factors seems to pertain to caste differences in household structure and to caste differences in family stress.

CASTE DIFFERENCES IN HOUSEHOLD STRUCTURE AND PERCEIVED MATERNAL ACCEPTANCE. The great majority (87 percent) of untouchable families in the Palashpur sample live in nuclear family households where mother and father live alone with their children. High-caste families, however, are evenly distributed between nuclear (50 percent) versus some form of extended family (50 percent) household.[7] This caste difference in living arrangements is statistically significant ($M = 7.58$, $p < .01$).

7. The category "extended family households" as used here includes "stem family households," "joint family households," and "extended (other) family households." Stem family households refer to households where a nuclear family lives with one or both paternal grandparents. Five high-caste families and one untouchable family live in this type of household. Joint family households refer to households where a man and his wife live with their children, his mother and/or father, plus his brother, brother's wife, and children. Only two sample families in Palashpur live in this type of household; one is a high-caste family and the other is an untouchable family. Finally, extended family (other) households refer to all types of extended family household that are not stem or joint. There are eight such households in the sample, seven high caste and one untouchable. All are some variant of a stem family household, with fathers' unmarried brother(s) or sister(s) also living in the household. Two high-caste children in the sample live in mother-child households, but no untouchable child lives in

Children's perceptions of maternal acceptance covary with the type of household in which they live. Specifically, children who live in nuclear family households, as do the great majority of untouchable children, report significantly more overall maternal acceptance (Child PARQ, $M = 104.23$) than do children who live in any form of extended family household, where half the high-caste children live (Child PARQ, $M = 118.50$; $t = 4.76$, $p < .001$). This difference in overall perceived maternal acceptance masks the fact that children living in nuclear family households differ from children living in extended family households primarily in their perceptions of maternal warmth and indifference/neglect, but not in hostility/aggression or undifferentiated rejection, as shown in table 6. There one can see that sample children in extended families report significantly less maternal warmth ($t = 4.96$, $p < .001$) and significantly more indifference and neglect ($t = 4.03$, $p < .001$) than do sample children in nuclear families.

These results are consistent with conclusions drawn both from northern India by Minturn and Lambert (1964) and from Orissa by Seymour (1983). That is, Minturn and Lambert found that maternal warmth among the Rajputs of Khalapur was lowest in extended family households (especially the joint family) and highest in nuclear family households. Seymour, too, found in Bhubaneswar that the mothers' positive affect increased regularly and substantially as one moved away from joint family households into nuclear family households. However, Seymour also found that when one considers collectively all caretakers of young children, expressions of positive affect increased as households increased in structural complexity from nuclear to extended. In the north India setting, Minturn and Lambert hypothesized that low maternal warmth in extended family households might be attributed to crowded, multifamily living arrangements with a minimum of privacy. In such households a greater amount of emotional control might be adaptive for minimizing interpresonal conflict. Perhaps the same mechan-

this type of household. The household composition of one sample untouchable family was undetermined. This caste distribution of family household types in Palashpur seems to be typical of much of West Bengal—indeed, of much of India—as described by Kolenda 1968.

TABLE 6 Perceived Maternal Acceptance-Rejection (Child PARQ) in Relation to Household Type in Palashpur

CHILD PARQ SCALE	EXTENDED FAMILY HOUSEHOLD (N = 16)		NUCLEAR FAMILY HOUSEHOLD (N = 30)			
	M	S.D.	*M*	S.D.	*t*	*p*
Low warmth	32.36	11.43	26.43	5.50	4.96	.001
Host./agg.	31.25	5.79	31.63	10.90	.23	n.s.
Indif./negl.	29.93	4.77	25.33	11.14	4.03	.001
Undif. rej.	19.88	5.25	21.03	8.79	-.32	n.s.

isms are at work in Palashpur, but other factors are also suggested later.

The type of extended family children live in is correlated significantly with perceived maternal warmth ($r = -.66$, $p < .01$): Children in stem family households (defined earlier in footnote 7) tend to perceive the least maternal warmth; children in joint family households (also defined in footnote 7) perceive intermediate maternal warmth; and children in other forms of extended family households (see footnote 7) perceive the most warmth. These results are unusual in that stem family households tend to be associated with maximum parental warmth and acceptance in most of the world (Rohner 1975). In Palashpur, however, the stem family may be associated with maximum stress—and therefore lowered warmth—for the young mother because, as we wrote in part 1, she is expected to be passively subordinate to her often domineering mother-in-law. Frequently her husband is more closely allied with his mother—the wife's mother-in-law—than with her, and her relationship with her father-in-law is apt to be somewhat distant and formal. As a result the mother has no other adult in the household to help diffuse tensions and possible conflict with the mother-in-law. The emotional distress associated with this potential tension and conflict may place mothers in Indian stem family households at a greater risk for withdrawing some of the warmth and affection they might otherwise express toward their children.

Evidence related to this speculation about the link between stress in stem family households and reduced maternal warmth is provided below, but first we should point out that even though children in nuclear family households experience more maternal warmth and acceptance than do children in extended (including stem) family households, children in high-caste nuclear families continue to report significantly less overall maternal acceptance (Child PARQ, $M = 116.61$) than do children in untouchable nuclear families (Child PARQ, $M = 105.17$; $t = -2.35$, $p < .05$). Apparently, then, factors other than household type per se are associated with caste differences in perceived maternal acceptance. Significant caste differences in the experience of family stress appear to be one such class of factors.

CASTE DIFFERENCES IN FAMILY STRESS AND PERCEIVED MATERNAL ACCEPTANCE. The higher the caste of a family in Palashpur the more stress it experiences in the sense that high-caste family members encounter deaths in the family ($r = .30$, $p = .039$) more often than do untouchable family members, and husbands and wives in higher-caste families experience serious physical or mental illness ($r = .30$, $p = .038$) more often than do spouses in untouchable families.[8] Also, high-caste families experience serious family conflict ($r = .27$, $p = .068$) and other serious problems ($r = .28$, $p = .056$) marginally more often than do untouchable families. Likely reasons for many of these caste differences in stress can be found in earlier chapters and are detailed more fully later.

This elevated level of stress in high-caste families seems to make mothers less warm and more overall rejecting (as reported on the PARQ by themselves as well as by their children) than mothers who do not live with such stress. More particularly—as shown in table 7, and as reported by mothers on the Mother PARQ as well as by children on the Child PARQ—mothers tend to be less warm in families where either spouse has suffered

8. No doubt high-caste families tend to experience death more often than untouchable families because high-caste villagers often live in extended family households that contain more people than do the nuclear family households of most untouchable families. With more people in the extended family household, the chances increase of someone dying, especially the elderly.

TABLE 7 Correlations between Individual Indicators of Family Stress and Perceived Maternal Acceptance (Child PARQ and Mother PARQ)

CHILD PARQ ($N = 47$)

Indicator of Family Stress	Warmth		Host./Agg.		Indif./Negl.		Undif. Rej.		Overall Rejection (Total PARQ)	
	r	p	r	p	r	p	r	p	r	p
Serious illness (physical or mental)	-.43	.003	.15	n.s.	.46	.001	.14	n.s.	.49	.00
Serious family conflict	-.42	.003	.06	n.s.	.45	.001	.31	.036	.49	.00
Other serious problems	-.08	n.s.	.29	.05	.05	n.s.	-.15	n.s.	-.07	n.s.

MOTHER PARQ ($N = 47$)

Indicator of Family Stress	Warmth		Host./Agg.		Indif./Negl.		Undif. Rej.		Overall Rejection (Total PARQ)	
	r	p	r	p	r	p	r	p	r	p
Serious illness (physical or mental)	-.37	.01	.03	n.s.	-.15	n.s.	.05	n.s.	.17	n.s.
Serious family conflict	-.48	.001	.04	n.s.	.13	n.s.	-.09	n.s.	.29	.05
Other serious problems	-.15	n.s.	.30	.04	.03	n.s.	.05	n.s.	.23	n.s.

serious physical or mental illness recently (Mother PARQ: $r = -.37$, $p = .01$; Child PARQ: $r = -.43$, $p = .003$) or where mothers live with serious family conflict (Mother PARQ: $r = -.48$, $p = .001$; Child PARQ: $r = -.42$, $p = .003$). Moreover, children perceive less overall maternal acceptance ($r = -.49$, $p < .001$)—and mothers tend to agree with this perception ($r = -.29$, $p = .05$)—insofar as either parent is involved in serious family conflict. Children also tend to perceive less overall maternal acceptance ($r = -.49$, $p = .001$) insofar as one or both parents have been seriously ill, physically or mentally.[9] Other significant correlations are also present in table 7.

Basic trends in the relationship between family stress and perceived maternal acceptance are simplified and clarified in table 9, where the three discrete indicators of family stress shown in table 7 are combined to create an overall Index of Family Stress. Before discussing results in table 9 we should indicate how the Family Stress Index was created. Table 8 shows that the three discrete indicators of family stress utilized in table 7 intercorrelate significantly with one another. Thus it is possible to sum the three stress scores for each family. Since each stress indicator is coded 1 = present (yes) or 2 = absent (no), a given family may have a Stress Index score ranging from 3 (where all three indicators of stress are absent) to 6 (where all three indicators of stress are present).[10] No family in the sample answered yes to all three indicators comprising the index (i.e., no index score achieved the possible upper limit of 6). The great majority of families scored 3 on the index (total sample $M = 3.33$, S.D. $= .75$, $N = 49$). Nonetheless, untouchable families experienced slightly but significantly less overall stress (Stress Index: $M = 3.00$, S.D. $= 0.00$) than did high-caste families ($M = 3.59$, S.D. $= .79$; $t = 2.98$, $p = .005$).

9. It is interesting to note that mothers tend to experience more physical and/or mental illness as adults to the degree that they experienced maternal hostility ($r = .29$, $p = .045$), undifferentiated rejection ($r = .32$, $p = .03$), or overall lowered maternal acceptance ($r = -.29$, $p = .043$) in their own childhoods.

10. The specific questions comprising indicators of family stress are: Have you or your husband experienced any of the following problems in the past year? (i) Serious physical or mental illness? (yes or no?) (ii) Serious family conflict (e.g., marital conflict)? (yes or no?) (iii) Other serious problems? (yes or no? If yes, please specify.)

TABLE 8 Intercorrelation of Indicators of Family Stress

	OTHER SERIOUS PROBLEMS	SERIOUS FAMILY CONFLICT
Serious illness (physical or mental)	.55***	.49***
Serious family conflict	.29*	

Note: $N = 49$.
*$p < .05$.
**$p < .01$.
***$p < .001$.

Caste differences in the experience of stress might be clarified somewhat by pointing out that 15 percent of the high-caste families experienced serious illness, including mental illness (one high-caste father was psychotic, for example), whereas only 4 percent of the untouchable families experienced this form of stress to a serious degree. Moreover, 19 percent of the mothers in high-caste families reported serious family conflict and "other serious problems," including, for example, insufficient money to provide dowry for unmarried daughters and physical conflict between sons and their alcoholic father. Only 4 percent of the untouchable mothers reported serious family conflict, and none cited the category of "other serious problems."

Reasons for caste differences in family conflict and "other" serious problems probably relate, in part, to the already discussed fact that high-caste women more often than untouchable women live in extended family households with sometimes domineering mothers-in-law, sometimes competitive sisters-in-law, or sometimes controlling elder brothers-in-law. One high-caste mother, for example, was upset because her elder brother-in-law and his wife refused to allow her to terminate an unwanted pregnancy from her psychotic husband. Other caste differences in family conflict seem to pertain to the fact that unhappy high-caste wives are only rarely able to leave their husbands, even—as noted earlier—if husbands abuse them physically. Untouchable wives suffer no such culturally sanctioned constraints.

Finally, caste differences in the frequency of serious illness may be due partly to differences in diet described in chapter 4. There we noted, for example, that untouchable women are usually healthy looking, whereas many high-caste women are not. This difference in physical appearance was attributed to the fact that, ironically, despite their extreme poverty, untouchable women commonly eat more nutritious foods than do high-caste women. Also, the physically active work life of untouchable women may contribute to their maintaining better physical health than the less physically active high-caste women.

Though the reasons for caste differences in stress may not always be understood with clarity, it seems that the Index of Family Stress correlates significantly with measures of perceived maternal acceptance-rejection, especially with maternal warmth and with overall maternal acceptance. That is, as shown in table 9, both children ($r = -.42$, $p = .003$) and their mothers ($r = -.45$, $p = .001$) agree that the greater the stress a family experiences (i.e., the higher the Stress Index score), the lower the maternal warmth shown toward children. Moreover, both children ($r = -.41$, $p = .004$) and their mothers ($r = -.31$, $p = .03$) agree that overall family stress is associated significantly with lowered maternal acceptance. Beyond this, children (but not mothers) report a significant connection between maternal indifference/neglect and the Index of Family Stress ($r = .44$, $p = .002$).

Sex Differences in Perceived Maternal Warmth

Up to this point we have concentrated primarily on caste differences in perceived maternal acceptance within Palashpur. Gender, however, is also an important predictor of variations in overall perceived acceptance, especially in perceived maternal warmth more specifically—as it is in much of India. Palashpur girls, for example, tend to perceive marginally less warmth (low warmth scale, $M = 31.04$) than do boys (low warmth scale, $M = 26.80$, $t = 1.79$, $p < .08$). The overall correlation between perceived warmth and children's sex is $r = .27$ ($p = .059$). Most of the sex differences in perceived maternal warmth in Palashpur, however, occur among high-caste chldren, not among untouchable children. That is, high-caste six- through twelve-year-old

TABLE 9 Correlations between Index of Family Stress and Perceived Maternal Acceptance-Rejection (Child PARQ and Mother PARQ)

PARQ SCALES AND TOTAL	CHILD PARQ		MOTHER PARQ	
	r	*p*	*r*	*p*
Warmth	-.42	.003	-.45	.001
Host./agg.	-.03	n.s.	.16	n.s.
Indif./negl.	.44	.002	.01	n.s.
Undif. rej.	-.15	n.s.	.01	n.s.
Overall rej. (Total PARQ)	.41	.004	.31	.03

Note: $N = 47$ for both Child PARQ and Mother PARQ.

girls perceive considerably less maternal warmth (low warmth, $M = 34.94$) than do the same-aged high-caste boys (low warmth, $M = 28.18$, $t = 1.96$, $p = .06$). Untouchable girls (low warmth, $M = 26.18$) and boys (low warmth, $M = 25.55$, $t = .07$, $p = .80$) perceive almost identical amounts of maternal warmth, which is, overall, somewhat more than that experienced by either boys or girls in high castes. We should note that these sex differences in perceived acceptance occur only on the warmth scale of the Child PARQ, not on the maternal hostility, neglect, or undifferentiated rejection scales, or on the overall (total) PARQ.

Several factors described in part 1 may help explain why high-caste girls in Palashpur report less maternal warmth than do high-caste boys, and especially less than either untouchable girls or boys. First, as explained earlier, high-caste girls—though loved by their parents—are nonetheless viewed as a liability, in part because of the sometimes onerous dowry demands associated with their future marriage. Moreover, when they move to their in-laws' homes these daughters are forever lost as economic contributors to their families of origin. An ancient Hindu aphorism stating that to raise a daughter is like watering another man's garden perhaps captures the essence of this latter point. High-caste boys, on the other hand, are not only wanted and favored but also needed, as explained in chapter 3, to assure the perpetuation of the patrilineage as well as to provide economic security to their aging parents, most often their mothers, and to light the funeral pyres of their deceased father. These and other factors appear to combine to perpetuate the widespread cultural preference in India for sons versus daughters (see Kakar 1978; Miller 1980, 1981; Poffenberger 1981).

As observed in part 1, untouchable families in Palashpur do not share this "male-preference" ideology to the same degree as high-caste families. Concomitantly one does not find the same gender differences in perceived maternal warmth among untouchable children. The partial absence of male preference among untouchables is perhaps associated with the fact that untouchable girls are not the liabilities girls are seen to be in high-caste families. Rather, from an early age untouchable girls are—as explained in chapter 4—major economic contributors; at marriage their parents could, until recently, demand payment from the groom's family for the loss of an economically productive family member. Unlike high-caste girls, untouchable girls often maintain strong, lifelong social, emotional, and sometimes economic ties with their families of origin.

Paralleling the gender differences in perceived maternal warmth among high-caste children in Palashpur is the tendency, noted in chapter 4, for high-caste families to distribute food unequally between the sexes, especially among older children. Sen and Sengupta (1983) found a similar trend for sex-linked inequalities in the distribution of food among children under the age of five years in two villages near Palashpur. The researchers found in these two villages that 46 percent of the high-caste and "scheduled caste" (i.e., untouchables plus some lower-ranking high castes) boys were malnourished to some degree, but 53 percent of the girls were malnourished. Gender within caste strata seemed to be an especially significant predictor of malnourishment for girls, no doubt for reasons similar to those described above. That is, 56 percent of the "scheduled caste" girls were somewhat malnourished, but only 50 percent of the high-caste girls were. Boys of both caste strata fared better than girls—only 46 percent of them were malnourished to a measurable degree. Not surprisingly, Sen and Sengupta found that the greater prevalence of undernourishment among girls was associated with greater deficits in their growth curves than in the growth curves of boys.

These gender-difference trends in food distribution and in perceived maternal warmth in the Palashpur area are consistent with the same trends in rural northern India as described by Miller (1981, 1983), Pettigrew (1986), and Poffenberger (1981). These authors noted that girls in rural northern India experience significantly greater neglect—sometimes to the point of death—than do boys. Parental neglect in this context refers to such matters as waiting longer before attending to girls' medical problems, investing fewer scarce family resources when a girl becomes ill, or providing girls with less preferred foods. It is not at all certain, however, that girls in northern India perceive this "neglect" as a form of rejection.

Age Differences in Perceived Maternal Acceptance

The child's age and the mother's age seem to be other significant but perhaps less important predictors of variations in perceived maternal acceptance in Palashpur. That is, even though neither boys nor girls in Palashpur perceived much age-related difference in maternal acceptance-rejection (beyond a slight tendency for children—both boys and girls—to report *less* undifferentiated rejection as they get older, from ages six through twelve; $r = -.27$, $p = .06$), mothers report differences in their behavior toward children, according to the age of the child. More specifically, mothers report on the Mother PARQ that they tend to be more indifferent and neglecting ($r = .44$, $p = .008$), perhaps more hostile and aggressive ($r = .29$, $p = .087$), and less overall accepting ($r = -.34$, $p < .05$) the older their children are (in the age range from six through twelve). But they do not report on the PARQ any age differences in their children on either the warmth scale or the undifferentiated rejection scale. We have no ready explanation for these age-related changes in maternal acceptance.

An intriguing concomitant to slight reductions in mothers' accepting behaviors toward older children is the fact that older mothers tend to report themselves as *more* accepting than do younger mothers. That is, older Palashpur-sample mothers, in relation to younger mothers, tend to report themselves on the PARQ as less hostile and aggressive toward their children ($r = -.30$, $p = .04$), less undifferentiated rejecting ($r = -.28$, $p = .059$, perhaps less indifferent and neglecting ($r = -.26$, $p = .08$), and more overall accepting (Mother PARQ: $r = -.32$, $p = .03$). Only maternal warmth is unaffected by a mother's age ($r = -.18$; $p =$ n.s.). (Sample mothers range in age from twenty to seventy years.) These age-related shifts in mothers' reported acceptance of their children may be, in part at least, a function of the fact that women's status in the Indian family–described in chapter 4–generally improves with increasing maturity (see also Fruzzetti 1982; Roy 1975, Seymour 1975).

Associated with this change in personal maturity and improved status are significant changes in mothers' personalities, changes that are also no doubt related to mothers' increasing acceptance of their children as the mothers get older. More specifically, as childless brides in their new husband's homes–often under the domination of their mothers-in-law–Palashpur women are, as noted in chapter 4, frequently at a lifetime low point in their status. But as shown earlier, this situation generally improves when they give birth to their first and subsequent children, especially if one or more of these offspring are boys. Their status generally continues to improve as they become mature senior wives, especially in high-caste families where the wives often live in joint family households. Over time their mothers-in-law begin to relinquish authority over them, and the wives–now mature women themselves, perhaps with daughters-in-law of their own–begin to reach ascendency within the family.

As we indicated above, personality changes tend to be associated with these changes in a mother's status and maturity. That is, as Palashpur mothers get older they tend to develop more positive feelings of self-esteem ($r = .32$, $p = .029$) and self-adequacy ($r = .43$, $p = .003$); they tend to become more stable emotionally ($r = .42$, $p = .004$); and their overall mental health status (as measured by the Adult PAQ, mother version) improves significantly ($r = .30$, $p = .039$). (A mothers' level of hostility/aggression, dependence, emotional responsiveness, and world-view do not vary significantly with age.) As we surmised, in all likelihood some portion of the reduction of maternal hostility/aggression, undifferentiated rejection, and perhaps indifference/neglect toward children can be explained by these improvements in a mother's feelings about herself as she grows older.

Summary of Perceived Maternal Acceptance and Its Effect and Determinants in Palashpur

This chapter has dealt with a considerable amount of technical information about the effects and determinants of perceived maternal acceptance in Palashpur. In this final section we summarize major conclusions drawn throughout the chapter.

We have indicated several times that India appears to be a land of significant contrasts in perceived maternal warmth and overall maternal acceptance, but in the village of Palashpur the great majority of children report their mothers to be warm, nonhostile, non-neglecting, and overall accepting. The same is said by mothers about their own mothers' treatment of them as children. Nonetheless, there are exceptions; at least a few children perceive themselves to be rejected by their mothers. And even among children who experience substantial maternal acceptance, some perceive more than others.

As predicted by PART's personality theory, variations in perceived maternal acceptance within Palashpur covary directly with variations in individuals' social-emotional functioning. That is, insofar as individuals perceive themselves to have been accepted as children by their mothers, they also tend to have positive feelings of self-esteem and self-adequacy, to be emotionally responsive and emotionally stable, to have a positive worldview, and to be nonhostile or nonaggressive. In Palashpur the relationships between perceived maternal acceptance and various personality dispositions were stronger for adults than for children, but this generational difference is probably attributable to the somewhat problematic psychometric characteristics of the Bengali-language version of the Child PAQ in relation to the more favorable characteristics of the equivalent versions of the Adult PAQ.

As we indicated above, Palashpur is like communities everywhere in showing a range of variation in perceived maternal warmth and overall acceptance. Caste and gender seem to be two of the most important determinants of differences in perceived maternal acceptance, but the child's age and the mother's age also appear to be significant in this respect. More specifically, the major caste-related contrast in maternal acceptance in Palashpur occurs among the high castes versus the untouchables: both children and mothers in high castes report less maternal warmth than do untouchable children and mothers; both children and mothers also agree that high-caste children experience slightly less overall maternal acceptance than do untouchable children. For some currently unexplained reason, these trends are reversed when Palashpur mothers reflect on their own childhoods. That is, untouchable mothers report having experienced slightly more hostility/aggression, indifference/neglect, and undifferentiated rejection, and less overall acceptance than did high-caste mothers in their childhoods. Women in the two caste strata do not differ significantly, however, in the amount of maternal warmth they report having received as children.

At least two classes of factors seem to help explain these caste differences in perceived maternal acceptance, namely, (1) caste differences in household structure and (2) caste differences in family stress. Regarding household structure, children who live in nuclear family households—as do almost all untouchable children—report significantly more overall maternal acceptance, more maternal warmth, and less indifference/neglect (but not more or less hostility/aggression or undifferentiated rejection) than do children who live in any form of extended family household, as do at least half the high-caste children. Those high-caste children who live in nuclear family households also report less overall maternal acceptance than do untouchable children living in such households. Evidently, then, factors other than household structure account for significant caste-based variations in perceived maternal acceptance.

The experience of family stress seems to be one such class of factors. Family stress is defined here as the experience of serious family conflict, the serious physical or mental illness of either the mother or the father, or other problems defined by the mother as seriously affecting either herself or her husband. Combining these indicators of stress into an overall Index of Family Stress, high-caste families were found to score significantly higher in stress than untouchable families; this greater experience of stress seemed to translate for high-caste families into slightly reduced maternal warmth and overall lowered maternal acceptance.

Gender, too, seems to be an important contributor to differences in perceived maternal warmth. Specifically, high-caste girls tend to report experiencing less maternal warmth than do either high-caste boys or untouchable children of either sex. Untouchable girls and boys, on the other hand, experience virtually the same degree of maternal warmth. These gender-related similarities and differences in the perception of maternal warmth among Palashpur's children—along with gender differences in the distribution of food to boys versus girls—seem to be consistent with reports that girls in rural, northern India experience significantly more parental neglect than do boys there. All these reported gender differences in parental behavior are probably related to the widely held cultural preference, in at least northern India, for sons over daughters.

Other portions of the variation in perceived maternal acceptance appears to be explained by the child's age as well as by the mother's. That is, as we wrote earlier, very young children typically seem to experience considerable maternal warmth and indulgence. Sometime between four and six, however, many parents begin to demand that their children show greater maturity; mothers report that they tend to be slightly but significantly more indifferent and neglecting, perhaps more hostile and aggressive, and certainly less overall accepting as their children mature from age six through twelve. Mothers do not, however, decrease the warmth they express toward their children during this time. Oddly, children themselves do not report experiencing these age-related changes in maternal behavior, beyond a slight tendency for them to report *less* undifferentiated rejection as they get older.

An interesting concomitant of these shifts in reported maternal behavior as children get older is the tendency for older mothers in Palashpur to report that they are less hostile and aggressive, less undifferentiated rejecting, perhaps less indifferent and neglecting, and more overall accepting than are younger mothers.

Maternal warmth is apparently unaffected by a mother's age. These age-related shifts in a mother's reported acceptance of children may be a function of the tendency for a mother's overall status within the family and community to improve with age; also, she may experience accompanying improvements in her social-emotional functioning. This at least is the expectation that one would normally derive from parental acceptance-rejection theory.

APPENDIX

Validity and Reliability of the Bengali-Language Versions of the PARQ and PAQ

Analyses of the validity and reliability of the Bengali-language versions of the Parental Acceptance-Rejection Questionnaire (PARQ) and the Personality Assessement Questionnaire (PAQ) were guided by standards outlined in the American Psychological Association's (1974) *Standards for Educational and Psychological Texts.* Analyses of the child versions of the self-report questionnaires are based on fifty six- through twelve-year-old children (with a mean age of 9.2 years) in the village of Palashpur. Twenty-three of the children were males, twenty-seven females. These children were taken from all caste groups in Palashpur and represent a reasonably stratified sample of village families with children in this age range. Analysis of the mother versions of the questionnaires are based on reports by mothers (or other major adult female caretakers) of these fifty children. Adult versions of the questionnaires draw from fifty-one of these women, and from seventeen of the children's fathers who were willing to respond to the questionnaires. Because of the severely attenuated sample of participating fathers, formal analysis of the father version of PARQ and PAQ will not be presented here. All questionnaires were written and administered in the Bengali language.

Bengali-language versions of the questionnaires were developed under the supervision of Chaki-Sircar, who is a native speaker of Bengali and is fluent in English. Chaki-Sircar translated the English-language version of the questionnaires into Bengali and then had a second bilingual speaker of Bengali and English "back-translate" (Brislin 1970, 1976) the questionnaires into English. The original English-language version was compared word for word with the back-translated version, and semantic discrepancies were noted. The process of translation/back-translation was repeated until the present versions of the Bengali-language questionnaires were created; they match quite closely the original English-language versions published in Rohner (1984). This report on the validity and reliability of the Bengali-language versions of the PARQ and PAQ may be compared with the English-language counterpart discussed in Rohner (1984).

Validity and Reliability of the Bengali-Language Versions of the PARQ

Three Bengali-language versions of the PARQ are presented here: (1) the Child PARQ asks children to reflect on the way their major caretakers (usually their mothers) treat them in terms of (*a*) perceived warmth/affection, (*b*) perceived hostility/aggression, (*c*) perceived indifference/neglect, and (*d*) perceived undifferentiated rejection. (Undifferentiated rejection refers to times when parents are perceived as withdrawing love from a child—i.e., the child interprets the parents' behavior as rejection—but where such rejection does not clearly reflect either parental hostility/aggression or indifference/neglect.) (2) The Mother PARQ asks the major caretaker (usually the mother) of each child to respond to the same items as on the Child PARQ, but from her own point of view. And (3) the Adult PARQ (mother version) asks these same caretakers (usually mothers) to reflect on the treatment they themselves received from their own parents in childhood.

In all versions of the PARQ, respondents assess parental behavior in terms of the same four scales noted above. The warmth/

affection scale contains twenty items, the hostility/aggression scale and the indifference/neglect scale each contains fifteen items, and the undifferentiated rejection scale contains ten items, for a total of sixty items. All versions of the PARQ are nearly identical except that the Adult PARQ (which asks respondents to reflect back on their own childhood) is written in the past tense whereas the other two versions are written in the present tense. Respondents are encouraged to respond the way they really feel, not the way they might (have) like(d) their parents to be or the way they might now like to be as parents themselves. Moreover, all versions of the PARQ utilize the same response format and scoring system, thus maximizing comparability across instruments. Ten to fifteen minutes are required to administer the PARQ. The higher the total test score one achieves on the PARQ, the more overall rejection the individual perceives in his or her family.

Table A.1 reveals the basic descriptive characteristics (i.e., scale means, standard deviations, the spread of subjects' responses to each scale, and the possible high and low scores for each scale) of the Bengali-language versions of the Child PARQ, Mother PARQ, and Adult PARQ (mother version) achieved by villagers in Palashpur. As shown in that table, mothers and children agree that, on the whole, children of Palashpur experience substantially more acceptance than rejection. Moreover, mothers tend to report themselves as having been accepted when they were children.

Reliability of the Bengali-Language Version of the PARQ

Cronbach's coefficient alpha (Nunnally 1967) was used as the principal measure of reliability of the Bengali-language version of the PARQ. Coefficient alpha is a conservative, lower-bound (Carmines and Zeller 1979) measurement of the internal consistency of items within a scale. A high alpha indicates that all items in a scale are sampling the same content area. As shown in table A.2, PARQ reliability coefficients (alphas) for scales on the Child PARQ spread from .46 to .87, with a median reliability of .71; alphas on scales of the Mother PARQ spread from .08 to .83, with a median reliability of .67; and alphas on scales of the Adult

TABLE A.1 Descriptive Statistics for Child, Mother, and Adult (Mother) PARQ Scales and Total PARQ Score, Bengali-Language Versions

SCALE		MEAN	S.D.	SUBJECTS' RESPONSES		POSSIBLE SCORES	
				Low	High	Lowest	Highest
Warmth[a]	Child	29.20	8.35	21	57	20	80
	Mother	27.54	5.89	20	50		
	Adult (mo.)	26.16	4.97	20	37		
Hostility	Child	31.32	5.76	17	41	15	60
	Mother	31.04	4.90	19	40		
	Adult (mo.)	26.49	7.93	15	43		
Indifference	Child	26.80	6.28	20	49	15	60
	Mother	25.56	3.91	17	33		
	Adult (mo.)	23.86	3.23	18	33		
Rejection (undif.)	Child	21.18	4.02	10	30	10	40
	Mother	23.64	2.72	16	29		
	Adult (mo.)	19.84	3.92	10	27		
Total PARQ	Child[b]	109.82	14.82	92	176	60	240
	Mother	107.76	11.82	78	134		
	Adult (mo.)	96.35	16.73	64	137		

Note: Child PARQ scores are based on $N = 50$; Mother PARQ scores are based on $N = 50$; Adult (mother) PARQ scores are based on $N = 51$.

a. Warmth scale-scores were reverse scored to make them a kind of "rejection" (i.e., "low warmth" or "coldness"). Therefore, the higher the warmth score the "colder" (less warm) the mother is perceived to be.

b. The total PARQ is keyed in the direction of rejection. Therefore, the higher the score the more the perceived rejection.

PARQ (mother version) spread from .52 to .87, with a median reliability of .81. Overall these data indicate that the various versions of the PARQ have adequate reliability. The warmth and indifference scales tend to be especially strong; the hostility scale is adequate; and the undifferentiated scale tends to be somewhat problematic, especially on the Mother PARQ. Why such variations occur among the various PARQ scales is not clear. However, average median reliability across all four scales for each version of the questionnaire tend to be acceptable, though not always ideal.

Validity of the Bengali-Language Version of the PARQ

A measure of the convergent validity of the Bengali PARQ and its constituent scales is provided by correlating the Child PARQ and its scales with the Mother PARQ and its scales.[1] Even though it has been demonstrated that parents and children do not necessarily view parental love, control, or discipline the same way (Schwarz, Barton-Henry, and Pruzinsky 1985; Michaels, Messé, and Stollack 1983; Serot and Teevan 1961; Zucker and Barron 1971), it seems reasonable to conclude that where parents and children do agree, independent confirmation has been provided about the accuracy of each party's reports on the parental behavior—and thus a significant element of convergent validity of reports has been provided.

In Palashpur, children and mothers agree to a substantial degree about maternal warmth ($r = .79$, $p < .001$) and to some degree about maternal indifference/neglect ($r = .29$, $p < .04$). They do not, however, agree significantly about maternal hostility/aggression ($r = .20$, $p = .17$) or about maternal undifferentiated/rejection ($r = -.01$, $p = .95$. Nonetheless, children and mothers do agree significantly about the *overall* level of parental acceptance-rejection shown children. That is, overall (total) Child PARQ scores correlate significantly ($r = .50$, $p < .0001$) with overall (total) Mother PARQ scores, thus providing a measure of convergent validity of mothers' and childrens' reporting of over-

1. Convergent validity implies that agreement exists between two different measures of a single construct or phenomenon.

TABLE A.2 Internal Consistency Reliability Coefficients (Alpha) for Bengali-Language PARQ Scales

VERSION OF THE PARQ	N	PARQ SCALE RELIABILITY (ALPHA) COEFFICIENT			
		Warmth/Affectn.	Host./Agg.	Indif./Negl.	Undif.Rej.
Child	49	.87***	.66***	.76***	.46***
Mother	50	.78***	.55***	.83***	.08
Adult (mo.)	47	.83***	.87***	.78***	.52***

*$p < .05$.
**$p < .01$.
***$p < .001$.

all acceptance-rejection. This point is worth highlighting in view of the tendency of some behavioral scientists to dismiss children's reports about their own experiences as unreliable and untrustworthy.

Additional evidence regarding the validity of the Bengali-language versions of the PARQ and their scales is provided by factor analysis. Factor analysis is a method for determining the number and nature of theoretically relevant clusters of variables (or "factors") underlying a larger number of variables. In this context, factor analyses of the various versions of the PARQ help one to ascertain the extent to which Bengali children and adults tend to group the sixty individual items on the PARQ into the four conceptual clusters of warmth, hostility/aggression, indifference/neglect, and undifferentiated rejection as postulated theoretically in parental acceptance-rejection theory (see Rohner 1980, 1986). In effect, factor analysis helps one answer the question Do Bengali-language versions of the PARQ measure the same phenomenon of parental acceptance-rejection that English-language versions are known to measure (see Rohner 1984)?

If the Palashpur villagers do not create consistent clusters of interrelated items in their responses to the PARQ, factor analysis will yield uninterpretable results. Or if villagers perceive different sets of relationships among PARQ's sixty items from those expected in PAR theory, then interpretable but different factors will emerge in factor analysis from the postulated ones. Both of these conditions would suggest strongly that Bengali-language versions of the PARQ are invalid for the purposes of this research; that is, they did not measure in Palashpur what they are supposed to measure. However, insofar as the same factors emerge in Palashpur as are expected theoretically in PAR theory, then supportive evidence of the construct validity of the Bengali-language versions of the PARQ is provided.

Since single-item reliability has been shown in psychometric theory to be low (Cronbach and Glesser 1953), in these analyses, items in PARQ scales were grouped into clusters of three to five items each, yielding sixteen subscores for each individual. The subscores were subjected to a principal components factor analysis. The resultant factor matrix was rotated to an oblique solution that fits better, according to Thurstone (1947), the de-

TABLE A.3 Factor Loading following Oblique Rotation of Data from Bengali-Language Version of the Child PARQ, Mother PARQ, and Adult PARQ (mother version)

PARQ SCALE ID	Cluster	FACTORS (CHILD) I (Accept.) Warmth	FACTORS (CHILD) II (Rejection) Indif./Negl.	FACTORS (CHILD) III (Rejection) Host. Rej.	FACTORS (MOTHER) I Indif./Negl.	FACTORS (MOTHER) II Warmth	FACTORS (MOTHER) III Host. Rej.	FACTORS (ADULT: MOTHER) I (Accept.) Warmth	FACTORS (ADULT: MOTHER) II (Rejection) Host. Rej.	FACTORS (ADULT: MOTHER) III (Rejection) Indif./Negl.
Warmth/affectn.	1	.97	.05	.17	.19	.85	.24	.77	.21	.12
	2	.90	.06	.05	.07	.78	.19	.89	.02	.19
	3	.89	.06	.00	.15	.76	.14	.80	.06	.20
	4	.86	.14	.01	.58	.02	.16	.93	.26	.06
	5	.92	.06	.00	.07	.68	.03	.90	.05	.05
Host./agg.	6	.08	.24	.71	.05	.26	.57	.09	.85	.02
	7	.34	.21	.58	.83	.11	.13	.04	.79	.19
	8	.29	.15	.68	.13	.12	.74	.09	.83	.04
	9	.64	.12	.30	.21	.05	.61	.14	.86	.15
Indif./negl.	10	.11	.95	.12	.82	.42	.15	.11	.12	.90
	11	.29	.83	.01	.90	.05	.18	.06	.12	.93
	12	.16	.87	.06	.93	.10	.11	.13	.03	.88
	13	.76	.12	.04	.34	.61	.17	.61	.28	.28

Undif. rej.	14	.22	.13	.89	.01	.15	.43	.09	.81	.06
	15	.22	.07	.60	.03	.20	.74	.20	.61	.32
	16	.68	.20	.31	.25	.52	.18	.65	.25	.24

Note: Prior to performing the factor analyses, warmth items on the PARQs were reverse scored, thereby transforming them into measures of maternal coldness (i.e., low warmth). For this reason clusters defining the warmth factor correlate positively with clusters defining the various rejection factors.

siderata for a simple-structure factor loading matrix. Table A.3 shows the matrix of factor loadings for the Bengali-language versions of the Child PARQ, Mother PARQ, and Adult PARQ (mother version).

As shown in Table A.3, the same three strong and theoretically interpretable factors emerged from factor analyses of all three versions of the PARQ. On both the Child PARQ and the Adult PARQ (mother version) a warmth (acceptance) factor emerged first, accounting for the greatest percentage of the variances among items in these two questionnaires. (The warmth factor is defined by high loadings with clusters 1–5, i.e., the PARQ warmth/affection scale.) The second factor to emerge on the Child PARQ is an indifference/neglect factor, defined by clusters 10–13 (i.e., the PARQ indifference/neglect scale). The third factor to appear on the Child PARQ is a factor labeled hostile rejection. This factor is defined by clusters 6–9 (i.e., the PARQ hostility/aggression scale) and 14–16 (i.e., the PARQ undifferentiated rejection scale).

The same results emerged on the other two versions of the PARQ, but the order of appearance varied. That is, the hostile rejection factor appeared second on the Adult PARQ (mother version), followed by the indifference/neglect factor. The indifference/neglect factor emerged first on the Mother PARQ, followed by a warmth factor and then the hostile rejection factor. These results are reassuring in that both children and adults in Palashpur seem to perceive the warmth (acceptance-rejection) dimension of parenting as PAR theory postulates and as assumed (but unmeasured) during the course of fieldwork. Thus additional supportive evidence is provided for the validity of the construct "perceived parental acceptance-rejection" in West Bengal, as measured by Bengali-language versions of the PARQ.

Validity and Reliability of the Bengali-Language Versions of the PAQ

Validity and reliability data for three Bengali-language versions of the PAQ are presented here: (1) the Child PAQ asks children to reflect on the seven personality dispositions described in chapter

6: (i) hostility and aggression, (ii) dependence, (iii) self-esteem, (iv) self-adequacy, (v) emotional responsiveness, (vi) emotional stability, and (vii) worldview. (2) The Mother PAQ asks mothers (or other caretakers) to reflect on the child's personality dispositions. And (3) the Adult PAQ (mother version) asks adults (mothers of the children, in this instance) to reflect on the same dispositions within themselves. The child and mother versions of the PAQ contain the same items designed to measure the seven personality clusters described above. Each of the seven scales contains six items. The Adult PAQ contains the same seven scales, but with nine items per scale. Vocabulary in the Child PAQ is simplified and more generalized than in the adult version. All versions of the PAQ utilize the same response options and scoring systems, thus maximizing direct comparability across different versions. Ten to fifteen minutes are required to administer the PAQ. The higher a total test score, the more impaired an individual's mental health or psychosocial functioning is thought to be.

Table A.4 reveals the basic descriptive characteristics (i.e., scale means, standard deviations, the spread of subjects' responses to each scale, and the possible high and low scores for each scale) of the Bengali-language versions of the Child PAQ, Mother PAQ, and Adult PAQ (mother version). Data in table A.4 show that, on the whole, children in Palashpur perceive themselves to be in fairly good mental health, as measured by the total Child PAQ score (M = 90.44). Mothers tend to agree with this perception, as determined from the Mother PAQ (M = 92.54). Mothers in Palashpur also seem to feel reasonably good about themselves, on the average, as shown by their Adult PAQ (mother version) mean score of 128.08. The reader must remember that the highest possible score on the Adult PAQ is 252, whereas the highest possible score on the Child and Mother PAQs is 168. Therefore the mother's Adult PAQ score of 128 is roughly equivalent to (or even a little lower than) the Child PAQ score of 90. Also, individual scale scores on all three versions of the PAQ vary considerably. In all three, dependence is the highest score and negative worldview is the lowest (i.e., children and adults in Palashpur tend to be dependent and they tend to have positive worldviews).

TABLE A.4 Descriptive Statistics for Child, Mother, and Adult (Mother) PAQ Scales and Total PAQ Scores, Bengali-Language Versions

SCALE		MEAN	S.D.	SUBJECTS' RESPONSES		POSSIBLE SCORES	
				Low	High	Lowest	Highest
Host./agg.	Child	13.00	2.73	6	17	6	24
	Mother	15.04	3.99	6	21	6	24
	Adult (mo.)	16.80	4.32	9	27	9	36
Dependence	Child	20.16	2.44	14	24	6	24
	Mother	20.60	2.20	13	24	6	24
	Adult (mo.)	26.08	3.42	18	31	9	36
Neg. self-est.	Child	11.50	2.70	6	19	6	24
	Mother	10.15	2.49	6	16	6	24
	Adult (mo.)	19.43	3.92	12	29	9	36
Neg. self-adeq.	Child	11.36	2.41	7	19	6	24
	Mother	11.25	2.74	6	20	6	24
	Adult (mo.)	17.35	3.98	10	29	9	36
Emo. unresp.	Child	10.58	2.79	6	17	6	24
	Mother	10.32	2.63	6	19	6	24
	Adult (mo.)	15.47	3.62	9	25	9	36

Emo. instab.	Child	14.86	3.44	6	20	6	24
	Mother	16.34	2.55	12	21	6	24
	Adult (mo.)	20.73	4.34	12	27	9	36
Neg. worldview	Child	8.92	2.54	6	14	6	24
	Mother	9.37	2.82	6	15	6	24
	Adult (mo.)	13.28	4.13	9	25	9	36
Total PAQ	Child	90.44	8.35	70	109	42	168
	Mother	92.54	8.45	77	113	42	168
	Adult (mo.)	128.08	16.42	97	160	63	252

Notes: Child PAQ scores are based on $N = 50$; Mother PAQ scores are based on $N = 50$; Adult (mother) PAQ scores are based on $N = 51$. PAQ scores are keyed in the direction of ''negative'' personality characteristics expected to be associated with perceived parental rejection. The higher the score the more impaired the level of psychosocial functioning is thought to be.

TABLE A.5 Internal Consistency Reliability Coefficients (Alpha) for Bengali-Language PAQ Scales

VERSION OF THE PAQ	N	PAQ SCALE RELIABILITY (ALPHA) COEFFICIENT						
		Host.	Dep.	Neg. Self-est.	Neg. Self-adeq.	Emo. Unresp.	Emo. Instab.	Neg. Worldview
Child PAQ	50	.11	.07	.39***	.25*	.46***	.57***	.54***
Mother PAQ	46	.60***	.56***	.23*	.25*	.25*	.37***	.44***
Adult PAQ (mo.)	33	.66***	.45***	.14	.55***	.53***	.25	.64***

*$p < .10$.
**$p < .05$.
***$p < .01$.

Reliability of the Bengali-Language Version of the PAQ

As with the PARQ, Cronbach's coefficient alpha was used as a measure of the reliability of the various versions of the PAQ. Table A.5 shows the reliability (alpha) coefficients for the Bengali-language versions of the Child, Mother, and Adult (mother version) PAQs. Alphas on scales of the Child PAQ spread from .07 to .57, with a median reliability of .39; alphas on scales of the Mother PAQ spread from .23 to .60, with a median reliability of .37; and alphas on scales on the Adult PAQ (mother version) spread from .14 to .66, with a median reliability of .55. Even though the majority of the alpha coefficients in table A.5 are statistically significant, many are far from ideal. No single personality variable stands out across all three versions of the PAQ as being especially problematic, however. Overall the Adult PAQ version of the Bengali-language edition of PAQ appears to be most psychometrically reliable, as assessed by coefficient alpha; the Bengali-language version of the Child PAQ appears here to be the most problematic.

Validity of the Bengali-Language Version of the PAQ

A measure of the convergent validity of the Bengali-language version of the PARQ was provided by correlating the Child PARQ and its scales with the Mother PARQ and its scales. The same may be done with the Child and Mother PAQs, but a serious caution must be introduced at this point. The PAQ is designed as a measure of an individual's subjective assessments of his or her own personality dispositions, dispositions such as self-esteem and self-adequacy that do not always have a directly observable manifestation. Hence to ask mothers to respond to the Mother PAQ is to ask mothers to make "best-guess" inferences about the way their children perceive themselves. Accordingly one could argue that correlation between Mother PAQ scales and Child PAQ scales is at best a weak estimate of convergent validity.

With these caveats in mind, one may see in table A.6 that few Mother PAQ scales correlate significantly with their counterparts on the Child PAQ: hostility/aggression, $r = .26$, $p = .06$; dependence, $r = .26$, $p = .07$; self-esteem, $r = .24$, $p = .11$; self-ade-

TABLE A.6 Correlation between and *t* Test of the Difference between Mother PAQ Scales (and Total PAQ) versus Child PAQ Scales (and Total PAQ), Bengali-Language Versions

PAQ	CHILD PAQ			MOTHER PAQ							
SCALE AND TOTAL	*M*	S.D.	*N*	*M*	S.D.	*N*	*r*	*p*	*t*	df	*p*
Host./agg.	13.00	2.73	50	15.04	3.99	50	.26	.06	-2.96	98	< .01
Dep.	20.16	2.44	50	20.60	2.19	50	.26	.07	-.94	98	ns
Neg. self-est.	11.50	2.70	50	10.15	2.49	48	.24	.11	2.57	96	< .02
Neg. self-adeq.	11.36	2.41	50	11.24	2.74	49	.03	.82	.006	97	ns
Emo. unresp.	10.58	2.79	50	10.32	2.63	50	.17	.25	.47	98	ns
Emo. instab.	14.86	3.44	50	16.34	2.55	50	.07	.65	-2.42	98	< .02
Neg. worldview	8.92	2.54	50	9.37	2.82	49	.50	.001	-.83	97	ns
Total PAQ	90.44	8.35	50	92.54	8.45	46	.23	.12	-1.22	94	ns

quacy, $r = .03$, $p = .82$; emotional responsiveness, $r = .17$, $p = .25$; emotional stability, $r = .07$, $p = .65$; worldview, $r = .50$, $p < .001$; total PAQ, $r = .23$, $p = .12$. Even though few scales on the two questionnaires correlate significantly, we should point out that table A.6 also shows that few mean scores on Mother PAQ scales are significantly different from mean scores on respective Child PAQ scales, thus indicating that mothers and children tend to agree on the relative level of children's individual personality dispositions and on the level of children's overall psychosocial functioning.

More specifically, mothers and children agree (i.e., t tests are not significantly different) on children's level of dependence ($t = -.94$, $p =$ n.s.), self-adequacy ($t = .006$, $p =$ n.s.), emotional responsiveness ($t = .47$, $p =$ n.s.), worldview ($t = -.83$, $p =$ n.s.), and overall mental health status (total PAQ $t = -1.22$, $p =$ n.s.). However, mothers perceive their children as being significantly more aggressive ($t = -2.96$, $p < .01$) and less emotionally stable ($t = -2.42$, $p < .02$) than children report themselves. Also, children have significantly less positive self-esteem than mothers think their children do ($t = 2.57$, $p < .02$). Nonetheless mothers and children agree more often than they disagree about children's personality dispositions, thus providing modest evidence about the convergent validity of the Bengali-language version of the Mother and Child PAQs.

Additional information regarding the validity of the Bengali-language versions of the PAQ and their scales is provided by factor analyses. The principal question addressed here is To what extent do Palashpur children and adults group items on the PAQ into the seven theoretically expectable clusters of hostility/aggression, dependence, self-esteem, self-adequacy, emotional responsiveness, emotional stability, and worldview? In effect, factor analysis helps one answer the question Do Bengali-language versions of the PAQ reported here measure the same seven personality dispositions that the English-language versions have been shown by Rohner (1984) to measure? Insofar as the same factors emerge in Palashpur as are expected theoretically in PAR theory, then suggestive evidence of the construct validity of the Bengali-language versions of the PAQ is provided.

As with factor analyses of the PARQ, factor analyses of the

TABLE A.7 Factor Loading following Oblique Rotation of Data from the Bengali-Language Version of the Child PAQ

PAQ SCALE ID	CLUSTER	FACTOR I NEG. EVAL. OF SELF & WORLD	FACTOR II EMO. INSTAB.	FACTOR III (UNINTERP.)	FACTOR IV (UNINTERP.)	FACTOR V EMO. UNRESP.
Host./agg.	1	.17	.27	.06	.91	.23
	2	.22	.27	.31	.20	.17
	3	.19	.07	.92	.10	.03
Dep.	4	.48	.46	.47	.20	.67
	5	.69	.56	.11	.22	.43
	6	.61	.58	.62	.13	.43
Neg. self-est.	7	.81	.32	.36	.26	.37
	8	.88	.19	.22	.26	.58
	9	.81	.26	.34	.27	.62
Neg. self-adeq.	10	.76	.38	.21	.13	.39
	11	.59	.06	.42	.50	.08
	12	.85	.10	.34	.22	.42
Emo. unresp.	13	.57	.33	.11	.42	.77
	14	.39	.15	.09	.21	.92
	15	.57	.29	.30	.27	.71
Emo. instab.	16	.17	.79	.19	.37	.16
	17	.28	.87	.11	.28	.33
	18	.29	.63	.25	.11	.68
Neg. worldview	19	.80	.11	.39	.35	.22
	20	.84	.04	.37	.45	.41
	21	.75	.07	.62	.38	.34

Child and Mother PAQs began by grouping the forty-two items on each of these PAQs into twenty-one clusters of two items each. Each set of three clusters corresponds to one PAQ scale (i.e., one personality disposition). Similarly, the sixty-three items on the Adult PAQ were grouped into twenty-one clusters of three items each. Again, each set of three clusters corresponded to one PAQ scale (i.e., one personality disposition). The clusters or subscores were subjected to a principal components factor analysis. The resultant factor matrix was rotated to an oblique solution. Tables A.7, A.8, and A.9 show the matrixes of factor loadings for the Bengali-language versions of the Child PAQ, Mother PAQ, and Adult PAQ (mother version), respectively. The criterion used to identify interpretable factors within each PAQ matrix was the requirement that at least two of the three clusters that define a given PAQ scale must load at .50 or higher on a factor.

By this criterion, three interpretable factors account for six of the seven scales on the Child PAQ, as shown in table A.7. The first factor, which may be called "Evaluation of Self and the World," is defined by high loadings (i.e., loadings at or above the criterion of .50) on two of the three dependence clusters, all three negative self-esteem clusters, all three negative self-adequacy clusters, two emotional unresponsiveness clusters, and all three negative worldview (i.e., negative evaluation of the world) clusters. The emotional unresponsiveness cluster, however, loads much more strongly on the last factor than on the first, so the last factor (Factor V) is labeled "Emotional Unresponsiveness." Similarly, two of the three dependence clusters load to criterion on the second factor (i.e., "Emotional Instability"), but not as strongly as on the first factor. As a result "dependence" is retained in the first factor, leaving Factor II to be defined strongly by all three emotional instability clusters. Factors III and IV are uninterpretable. The only Child PAQ scale that does not emerge in this factor analysis is hostility/aggression, but one of its clusters loaded strongly (i.e., above .90) on each of the uninterpretable factors, III and IV.

Overall it appears that children in Palashpur perceive the personality dispositions postulated in PAR theory (as measured in the Child PAQ)—with the possible exception of hostility/aggression. These children do not, however, seem to discriminate clearly

TABLE A.8 Factor Loading following Oblique Rotation of Data from the Bengali-Language Version of the Mother PAQ

PAQ SCALE ID	CLUSTER	FACTOR I DEPENDENT UNRESP.	FACTOR II HOST./ AGG.	FACTOR III NEG. WORLDVIEW	FACTOR IV EMO. INSTAB.	FACTOR V (UNINTERP.)	FACTOR VI NEG. SELF-EST.	FACTOR VII NEG. SELF-ADEQ.
Host./agg.	1	.13	.89	.24	.22	.49	.07	.22
	2	.24	.36	.28	.10	.92	.09	.18
	3	.13	.93	.05	.30	.30	.28	.15
Dep.	4	.73	.33	.40	.60	.41	.54	.46
	5	.73	.17	.53	.57	.46	.53	.53
	6	.61	.35	.41	.67	.56	.39	.41
Neg. self-est.	7	.38	.27	.10	.29	.07	.90	.43
	8	.82	.08	.20	.43	.01	.65	.42
	9	.43	.13	.32	.31	.21	.83	.34
Neg. self-adeq.	10	.44	.09	.44	.37	.10	.42	.89
	11	.55	.35	.03	.25	.29	.43	.80
	12	.82	.21	.34	.28	.28	.34	.59
Emo. unresp.	13	.87	.13	.50	.41	.30	.30	34
	14	.65	.20	.47	.31	.16	.56	.58
	15	.52	.30	.44	.26	.24	.58	.58
Emo. instab.	16	.07	.61	.14	.44	.64	.26	.06
	17	.29	.40	.08	.81	.18	.53	.40
	18	.43	.22	.30	.90	.15	.20	.25
Neg. worldview	19	.49	.11	.87	.23	.27	.33	.32
	20	.52	.34	.74	.50	.15	.29	.57
	21	.46	.15	.88	.24	.37	.30	.34

some dispositions from others, for example, self-esteem from self-adequacy, worldview, or dependence. Self-esteem and self-adequacy are closely linked theoretically, and they often emerge in international research as an undifferentiated "Self-Evaluation" factor. However, worldview and especially dependence are not usually expected to appear in the same factor with self-esteem and self-adequacy. Thus equivocal evidence is provided here for the construct validity of the Bengali-language version of the Child PAQ. The lack of clarity in the factor structure of this version of the Child PAQ is partly explained by the low alpha coefficients of the "hostility/aggression" and "dependence" scales, indicating limited internal consistency among these scales as perceived by Bengali children. Several different factor analyses were performed in an attempt to clarify these ambiguities, but none yielded a clearer factor structure than the one reported here.

Factor analyses of the Bengali-language versions of the Mother PAQ and the Adult PAQ (mother version) show clearer and more differentiated factor structures. Factor structure for the Mother PAQ is shown in table A.8. There one can see that six interpretable factors account for all seven PAQ scales. More specifically, Factor I ("Dependent Emotional Unresponsiveness") is defined by high loadings on all three clusters defining both the dependence scale and the emotional unresponsiveness scale. The factor is also defined by criterion-level loadings from two of the negative self-adequacy clusters. But overall the clusters for this scale load much higher on Factor VII, which, accordingly, takes the name "Negative Self-Adequacy" factor. Factor II ("Hostility/Aggression") is defined strongly by two clusters on the hostility/aggression scale, and Factor III ("Negative Worldview") is defined unambiguously by all three clusters of the negative worldview scale. Factor IV ("Emotional Instability") is defined by strong loadings on two clusters of the emotional instability scale. Dependence also loads to criterion on this factor, but since the dependence-scale clusters load more strongly on Factor I, it is retained with that factor. Factor V is uninterpretable. Factor VI ("Negative Self-Esteem") is defined principally by the three clusters on the negative self-esteem scale, but two of the dependence-scale clusters and two of the emotional unresponsiveness

TABLE A.9 Factor Loading following Oblique Rotation of Data from the Bengali-Language Version of the Adult PAQ (mother version)

PAQ SCALE ID	CLUSTER	FACTOR I EMO. UNRESP./ NEG. WORLDVIEW	FACTOR II EMO. INSTAB.	FACTOR III HOST./AGG.	FACTOR IV (UNINTERP.)	FACTOR V NEG. SELF-EVAL.	FACTOR VI DEP.
Host./agg.	1	.27	.58	.39	.42	.33	.18
	2	.23	.26	.50	.76	.03	.11
	3	.07	.16	.96	.17	.03	.12
Dep.	4	.41	.42	.21	.10	.39	.88
	5	.24	.36	.01	.34	.42	.82
	6	.53	.26	.10	.12	.53	.71
Neg. self-est.	7	.21	.29	.02	.19	.92	.43
	8	.85	.09	.36	.13	.49	.56
	9	.02	.78	.30	.18	.41	.39
Neg. self-adeq.	10	.56	.29	.04	.01	.88	.29
	11	.78	.20	.27	.23	.65	.54
	12	.59	.54	.04	.05	.79	.50
Emo. unresp.	13	.81	.29	.08	.15	.42	.50
	14	.87	.15	.10	.14	.37	.17
	15	.68	.24	.17	.23	.42	.33
Emo. instab.	16	.48	.49	.18	.05	.53	.70
	17	.04	.87	.14	.25	.20	.26
	18	.53	.62	.04	.11	.50	.62
Neg. worldview	19	.38	.37	.07	.73	.42	.40
	20	.85	.01	.27	.12	.47	.51
	21	.83	.10	.24	.04	.54	.47

clusters also load to criterion here. As noted earlier, however, both of the latter scales load more strongly on Factor I and are therefore retained there. Finally, as already observed, Factor VII ("Negative Self-Adequacy") is defined by all three clusters on the negative self-adequacy scale. Thus reasonably strong evidence regarding the construct validity of the Bengali-language version of the Mother PAQ is provided by this factor analysis.

Five interpretable factors account for all seven scales of the Adult PAQ (mother version), as shown in table A.9. Factor I ("Emotional Unresponsiveness/Negative Worldview") is defined by all three clusters of the emotional unresponsiveness scale and by two clusters of the negative worldview scale. All three clusters of the negative self-adequacy scale also load to criterion on this factor, but since the clusters load even more strongly on Factor V they are retained there. Factor II ("Emotional Instability") is clearly defined by all three clusters of the emotional instability scale, and none other. Similarly, Factor III ("Hostility/Aggression") is defined solely by two clusters of the hostility/aggression scale. Factor IV is uninterpretable. Factor V ("Negative Self-Evaluation") is defined by two clusters (one of which loads marginally at .49) of the negative self-esteem scale, and all three clusters of the negative self-adequacy scale. Two clusters of the emotional instability scale also load to criterion on this factor. But they load even more strongly on Factor II, and so they are retained there. Finally, Factor VI ("Dependence") is defined by all three clusters of the dependence scale. Two clusters of the negative self-adequacy scale also load to criterion on this factor, but since they load more strongly on Factor V they are retained there. As with factor analysis of the Mother PAQ, factor analysis of the Bengali-language version of the Adult PAQ (mother version) provides moderately strong evidence regarding the construct validity of the theoretical constructs underlying the Adult PAQ scales.

Taken in the aggregate, evidence provided here suggests that even though the Bengali-language versions of the PARQ and PAQ are sometimes far from ideal, both sets of self-report questionnaires have sufficient psychometric reliability and validity to be used with reasonable confidence on samples of Bengali-speaking children and adults.

Glossary of Bengali Terms

Adhikari. A Brahman of lower rank.

Akacha. Clothing that has been polluted by contact with other people, especially untouchables. Literally, "unwashed."

Alpana. Traditional designs used as decorations for festivals.

Ardhanareesvar. The Hindu god who is man on the right half and woman on the left; a representation of Siva and his consort Parvati.

Asura. The embodiment of evil and beastly power.

Aswin. Bengali month between September and October.

Bagal. A young *mahinder.*

Bamon-kakima. Brahman aunt (father's sister).

Bamonpara. A section of Palashpur where the Brahmans live.

Banesvar. The second day of Dharmapuja festival; also, an alternate name for the god Siva.

Banyan. An east Indian tree of the mulberry family, whose branches send out shoots that grow into the soil and root to form secondary trunks.

Barga. Sharecropping system in which contracts are renewed annually.

Bargadari. Land tenure system in which the cultivator has power of veto and/or the possibility of compensation in the transfer of farming rights, or in selling land under cultivation by the landowner.

Barjatri. The groom's entourage at a wedding.

Barojat. "Superior caste."

Baro jyatha. Father's oldest brother.

Bhadra-Aswin. The month between August and September.

Bhadralok. "Civilized" (i.e., literate, proper, or genteel) people.

Bhadu. Festival of the untouchables, celebrating the affection of fathers for unmarried daughters.

Bhagchasi. Economic system where the landowner receives 55 percent of the crop, or twenty-two tins (i.e., large kerosene cans) of paddy. The cultivator gets eighteen cans.

Bhajo. A festival of the untouchables.

Bhaktibad. Vaisnava school of Hindu religion.

Bhaktya. A Lohar, Handi, or Dom devotee of Dharmaraj.

Bhat. Rice.

Bhatar. Husband.

Bhattacharyya. A subgroup within the Brahman caste.

Bigha. A unit of land where two-and-one-half *bighas* equal one acre, or alternatively, one *bigha* is equivalent to approximately four-tenths of an acre.

Birbhum. The district of West Bengal in which Palashpur is situated.

Bolan. Group singing of devotional songs by untouchable men. The songs describe the romantic union of Lord Krishna and his consort, Radha.

Brata. Various Bengali rituals observed by women.

Burorai. A holy location in Palashpur believed to be the place of origin of the deity Dharma.

Chaitra. The Bengali month between March and April.

Chandrai. A deified legendary hero from the Dom caste.

Chhotojat. "Inferior caste."

Chhotolok. Illiterate, "uncivilized" people.

Chhutor. Carpenter caste.

Chintamoni. A Manasha image, or image of the snake goddess.

Dada. Older brother.

Dadamashai. Maternal grandfather; also *dadu*.

Dadu. Maternal grandfather; also *dadamashai* or *thakurdada.*

Deepa bali. The festival of lights.

Devatta. Land dedicated to the goddess Dhanika Chandi. Income from *devatta* is contributed to the annual feast celebrating the goddess.

Dhak. Large (fifty-to-sixty-pound) drum played by Baen men during Dharmapuja and other ritual occasions.

Dhanputni. A rice transplanter, usually female.

Dharam sarkar. Political body associated with the principal deity of the village, Dharmaraj.

Dharmapuja. April festival worshiping the village deity, Dharmaraj.

Dharmaraj. The village deity within Palashpur.

Dhoti. White garment with or without colored borders, worn by males. The male counterpart to the female sari.

Dida. Maternal grandmother; also *didima* or *thakurma.*

Didi. Elder sister.

Didima. Maternal grandmother; also *dida.*

Dom. An untouchable caste; those who cremate dead bodies.

Doob. Ritual immersion (cleansing) of the head and body into the water of a pond or river.

Durga. The goddess of strength and power.

Durgapuja. A four-day worship of the goddess Durga.

Dwija. Literally "twice-born." Refers to the *upanayana* rite of Brahman boys.

Ganesha. The god of business and success, and god of the common people in Palashpur.

Gatar. One's body or strength.

Gharer-Laxmi. Daughter-in-law.

Ghee. Clarified butter fat.

Gopi. A milkmaid of Vrindavana, the legendary abode of the young Lord Krishna.

Gotra. Subgroup within a caste.

Gram panchayat. Formal governing body of the village, working under the district and state administration.

Gram sabha. Administrative body overseeing numerous villages.

Gurudeva. A teacher.

Hadudu. A game played by groups of children.

Handi. An untouchable caste.

Holi. Festival of colors.

Indra. A Vedic god of rain.

Jaggery. Unrefined brown sugar.

Jalchal. The castes from whom one may accept water.

Jam. A type of edible fruit coming from the *jam* tree.

Jathtuto. Children of father's elder brother.

Jati. Caste.

Jatra. All-night plays performed by professional groups.

Jyatha. Father's elder brother, and his age-mates.

Kacha. Unpolluted (literally, "washed") clothing untouched by untouchables.

Kachu. Root vegetable of the Arum family.

Kaka. Fictive "uncle." Term applied to father's age-mates (versus men older than father).

Kakima. Father's sister (paternal aunt).

Kali. Goddess who is the destroyer of all evil.

Kalipuja. The worship of Mother Kali.

Kali *tala.* The place in Palashpur where the Kali temple has been erected.

Kaliyuga. One of four time periods or Yugas in Hindu mythology. Kaliyuga is the "dark age," or contemporary times.

Kalurai. A deified legendary hero from the Dom caste.

Kamala. Literally "one who sits on a lotus." Another name for Laxmi.

Kanyadan. The gift of a virgin bride from the girl's father to the groom.

Kartikeya. The god of war.

Khurtuto. Children of father's younger brother.

Kirshani. An economic system where the cultivator receives one-third of the crop from the landowner, and the landowner provides the needed agricultural equipment.

Laxmi. Goddess of grace and prosperity worshiped at home.

Laxmipuja. Worship of the goddess Laxmi, observed immediately following Durgapuja.

Loharpara. Section of Palashpur where the Lohar live.

Loongi. Saronglike clothing worn by men.

Ludo. A board game like Parcheesi.

Ma. "Little mother"; also a feminine suffix.

Madal. A small drum.

Ma Durga. Supreme goddess of strength, and destroyer of evil.

Mahabharata. One of the two Indian religious epics.

Mahamila. Literally, "the great women." Used in reference to female *bhaktyas.*

Mahinder. Economic relationship of untouchable males serving their high-caste employers, usually for life.

Mahisharma. The buffalo demon.

Majhis. Local name for the Santal tribe.

Mama. Mother's brother (maternal uncle).

Manib. High-caste "master," or employer.

Manasha. Devotional songs of motherhood; also the snake goddess.

Mashima. Mother's sister.

Meghrai. The Lord of Clouds; also, a holy location on the southwestern outskirts of Palashpur.

Mejo kaka. Father's younger brother.

Mosh-chora. An untouchable child's game of riding a water buffalo.

Muchipara. A section of Palashpur where the Muchi live.

Muktadhar. A holy pond on the outskirts of Palashpur.

Nagda system. Daily wage labor.

Napit. Barber caste; one of the Sudra castes.

N.P. A form of currency (Nave Paise) where 100 *N.P.* equals one rupee.

Orey bhai suno. Literally, "Oh brother, listen to me." A refrain for verses recited during the worship of Manasha.

Palash. A large tree growing around Palashpur, with bright red flowers.

Pattadari system. Government land rented for a small fee to landless untouchable men to cultivate.

Paschimpara. Western ward of Palashpur.

Phoolsajya. The bed in the bridal chamber, which is decorated with flowers.

Pishima. Father's sister (paternal aunt).

Pishtuto. Children of father's sister (paternal cousins).

Pradhan. Chief political representative of the *panchayat.*

Prasad. Food that has been offered to a deity.

Pubpara. Eastern ward of Palashpur.

Puja. Any of several Bengali religious "worships" such as Durgapuga and Kalipuja.

Rabisasya. Winter crops (or sun-ripened crops), for example mustard seed, potatoes, and sugarcane.

Raktabeeja. Literally, "offspring who emanate from every drop of blood." Used in referring to Asura.

Ramayana. One of the two Indian religious epics.

Ruppur gram panachayat. A political body of *gram sabha* representatives from five *gram sabhas.*

Sanga. Arrangement for remarriage of a young untouchable widow.

Sanjpujani brata. Women's "evening worship" ritual performed at sunset.

Sanskrit. A former (now dead) language of India in which the religious epics were composed.

Santal. Local tribal people.

Saraswati. Goddess of learning, wisdom, art.

Saraswatipuja. Worship of Saraswati performed by schoolchildren in January.

Satgoppara. A section of Palashpur where the Satgop live.

Sati. Literally, "good woman." A now illegal custom in which Hindu widows cremated themselves on their deceased husbands' funeral pyres.

Shakti. Spiritual energy of women associated with their suffering and self-abnegation. Feminine manifestation of the power of the Supreme Being, Mother Durga.

Shraddha. Funeral rites.

Shravana. The Bengali month between July and August.

Sindur. Vermillion powder placed as a dot on the forehead of women and used by women in the part of their hair. Signifies a married woman.

Siva. Mother Durga's husband. The god of destruction and regeneration.

Sivaratri *brata.* Annual feasting and worship of Lord Siva.

Tal. Palm fruit.

Tambulipara. The section of Palashpur where the Tambuli live.

Thakurdada. Maternal grandfather; also *dadu.*

Thakurma. Maternal grandmother; also *dida.*

Thika. Economic system where the landowner receives a fixed rent in the form of paddy. Surplus paddy goes to the cultivator.

Upanayana. The "sacred thread rite," that is, the puberty rite for adolescent Brahman boys.

Upa-pradhan. Elected chief of the village administrative body, and local representative to the *gram sabha.*

Vaisnava. Worshipers of Lord Vishnu. One school of high-caste Hindu religious philosophy.

Vaisnavite. Followers of Lord Vishnu (Krishna).

Vrindavana. The legendary home of Lord Krishna when he was a young cowherd.

Yama. The immortal god of death.

Yamuna. Yama's sister.

Zamindari. The system of landholding and revenue collection by *zaminders.* Also, the land held or administered by a *zaminder,* that is, a feudal landlord paying the government a fixed revenue.

References

Ali, Amir H. 1960. *Then and now (1933–58)*. Calcutta: Asia Publishing House.

American Psychological Association. 1974. *Standards for educational and psychological tests*. Washington D.C.: American Psychological Association.

Arnold, Fred, Rodolfo A. Bulatao, Chalio Buripakdi, Betty J. Chung, James T. Fawcett, Toshio Iritani, Sung Jin Lee, and Tsong-shien Wu. 1975. *The value of children: A cross-national study*. Vol. 1. *Introduction and comparative analysis*. Honolulu: East-West Center.

Ausubel, David, E. E. Balthazar, I. Rosenthal, L. S. Blackman, S. H. Schpoont, and J. Welkowitz. 1954. Perceived parent attitudes as determinants of children's ego structure. *Child Development* 25:173–83.

Bennett, Lynn. 1983. *Dangerous wives and sacred sisters: social and symbolic roles of high-caste women in Nepal*. New York: Columbia University Press.

Brislin, Richard. 1970. Back-translation for cross-cultural research. *Journal of Cross-Cultural Psychology* 1:185–216.

———. 1976. *Translation: Applications and research*. New York: Wiley/Halsted.

Carmines, Edward G., and Richard A. Zeller. 1979. *Reliability and validity assessment*. Sage University Paper Series on Quantitative Applications in the Social Sciences, 07–017. Beverly Hills, Calif.: Sage Publications.

Carstairs, G. 1957. *Twice born*. London: Hogarth Press.

Chaki-Sircar, Manjusri. 1973. The worship of mother-goddess and the Bengali socialization process. Paper written as partial requirement for preliminary certification, Department of Anthropology, Columbia University.

———. 1980. Widowhood among the uppercaste Hindus: A legacy of sati. Paper.

Cook, Alicia S. 1984. India's working children. *Horizons,* Winter.

Cronbach, L. J., and G. C. Glesser. 1953. Assessing similarity between profiles. *Psychological Bulletin* 50:456–73.

Davis, Marvin. 1976. The politics of family life in rural West Bengal. *Ethnology* 15:189–200.

Ember, Carol R. 1983. The relative decline in women's contribution to agriculture with intensification. *American Anthropologist* 85:285–304.

Erikson, Erik. 1969. *Ghandi's truth.* New York: W. W. Norton.

Fruzzetti, Lina M. 1982. *The gift of a virgin: Women, marriage and ritual in a Bengali society.* New Brunswick, N.J.: Rutgers University Press.

Goldin, Paul C. 1969. A review of children's reports on parent behavior. *Psychological Bulletin* 71:222–36.

Goody, Jack, and S. J. Tambiah. 1973. *Bridewealth and dowry.* Cambridge: Cambridge University Press.

Government of India. 1974. *Towards equality.* Report of the Committee on the status of Women in India. New Delhi: Department of Social Welfare, Ministry of Education and Social Welfare.

Haldar, Gopal. 1954. *Bangla Sahityer Ruprekha* (Sketches of Bengal literature). Calcutta: A. Mukherjea and Co.

Harper, Edward B. 1969. Fear and the status of women. *American Anthropologist* 25:81–95.

Heilbrun, Alfred B., Jr. 1973. *Aversive maternal control: A theory of schizophrenic development.* New York: John Wiley.

Inden, Ronald B. 1976. *Marriage and rank in Bengali culture: A history of caste and clan in middle-period Bengal.* Berkeley: University of California Press.

Inden, Ronald B., and Ralph W. Nicholas. 1977. *Kinship in Bengali culture.* Chicago: University of Chicago Press.

Kakar, Sudhir. 1978. *The inner world: A psycho-analytic study of childhood and society in India.* Delhi: Oxford University Press.

———. 1979. Childhood in India: Traditional ideals and contemporary reality. *International Social Science Journal* 31:444–56.

Klass, Morton. 1966. Marriage rules in Bengal. *American Anthropologist* 68:951–70.

Kolenda, Pauline M. 1968. Region, caste and family structure: A comparative study of the Indian "joint" family. In Milton Singer and Bernard S. Cohn, eds., *Structure and change in Indian society,* pp. 339–96. Chicago: Aldine Publishing.

Lannoy, R. 1971. *The speaking tree: A study of Indian culture and society.* New York: Oxford University Press.

Marriott, McKim. 1955. Little communities in an indigenous civilization. In McKim Marriot, ed., *Village India,* pp. 171–222. Chicago: University of Chicago Press.

Michaels, Gerald Y., Larry A. Messé, and Gary E. Stollack. 1983. Seeing parental behavior through different eyes: Exploring the importance of person perception processes in parents and children. *Genetic Psychology Monographs.* 107:3–60.

Miller, Barbara D. 1978. Sexual discrimination and population dynamics in rural India. Ph.D. dissertation. Syracuse University.

———. 1980. Female juvenile mortality in rural India. *Eastern Anthropologist* 33:19–37.

———. 1981. *The endangered sex: Neglect of female children in rural north India.* Ithaca, N.Y.: Cornell University Press.

———. 1983. Son preference, daughter neglect, and juvenile sex ratio: Pakistan and Bangladesh compared. Working paper no. 33. Michigan State University.

Minturn, L., and J. Hitchcock. 1966. *The Rajputs of Khalapur, India.* New York: John Wiley.

Minturn, L., and W. W. Lambert. 1964. *Mothers of six cultures: Antecedents of child rearing.* New York: John Wiley.

Mitra, Amalendu. 1972. *Rarher Sanskriti.* Calcutta: Firma K. L. Mukhapodhaya.

Nag, Moni, B. N. F. White, and R. C. Peet. 1978. An anthropological approach to the study of the economic value of children in Java and Nepal. *Current Anthropology* 19:293–306.

Narain, D. 1964. Growing up in India. *Family Process* 3:148–54.

Nunnally, J. C. 1967. *Psychometric theory.* New York: McGraw-Hill.

Ostor, Akos. 1984. *Culture and power: Legend, ritual, trade and revolution in a Bengali society.* Beverly Hills, Calif.: Sage Publications.

Pettigrew, Joyce. 1986. Child neglect in rural Punjabi families. *Journal of Comparative Family Studies.* 17:63–85.

Piggott, Stuart. 1960. *Some ancient cities of India.* London: Oxford University Press.

Poffenberger, Thomas. 1981. Child rearing and social structure in India: Toward a cross-cultural definition of child abuse and neglect. In J. Korbin, ed., *Child abuse and neglect: Cross-cultural perspectives.* Berkeley: University of California Press.

Potvin, Raymond H. 1977. Adolescent god images. *Review of Religious Research* 19:43–53.

Rabkin, L. Y. 1965. The patient's family: Research methods. *Family Process* 4:105–32.

Rohner, Evelyn C., and Ronald P. Rohner. 1975. They love me not: Psychological effects of rejection. In R. P. Rohner, *They love me, they love me not,* chap. 3. New Haven, Conn.: HRAF Press.

Rohner, Ronald P. 1975. *They love me, they love me not: A worldwide study of the effects of parental acceptance and rejection.* New Haven, Conn.: HRAF Press.

———. 1980. Worldwide tests of parental acceptance-rejection theory: An overview. *Behavior Science Research* 15:1–21.

———. 1984. *Handbook for the study of parental acceptance and rejection.* Center for the Study of Parental Acceptance and Rejection, University of Connecticut.

———. 1986. *The warmth dimension: Foundations of parental acceptance-rejection theory.* Beverly Hills, Calif.: Sage Publications.

Rohner, Ronald P., and Caroline C. Nielsen. 1978. *Parental acceptance and rejection: A review and annotated bibliography of research and theory.* 2 vols. New Haven, Conn.: HRAFlex Books.

Rohner, Ronald P., and Evelyn C. Rohner, eds. 1980. Worldwide tests of parental acceptance-rejection theory. Special issue, *Behavior Science Research,* no. 15.

Roland, Alan. 1982. Toward a psychoanalytical psychology of hierarchical relationships in Hindu India. *Ethos* 10:232–53.

Roy, Manisha. 1975. *Bengali women.* Chicago: University of Chicago Press.

Schwarz, J. Conrad, Marianne L. Barton-Henry, and Thomas Pruzinsky. 1985. Assessing child rearing behaviors: A comparison of ratings made by mother, father, child and sibling on the CRPBI. *Child Development* 56:462–79.

Sen, Amartya and Sunil Sengupta. 1983. Malnutrition of rural children and the sex bias. *Economic and Political Weekly* (May):855–64.

Sen, Sukumar. 1948. *Banga Sahityer Idihas* (History of Bengali literature). Calcutta: Manashi Press.

Sengupta, A. K. 1955. *Parama Prakriti Saradamani.* Calcutta: Signet Press.

Serot, N., and R. Teevan. 1961. Perception of the parent-child relationship and its relation to child adjustment. *Child Development* 32:373–78.

Seymour, Susan. 1975. Some determinants of sex roles in a changing Indian town. *American Ethnologist* 4:757–69.

———. 1976. Caste/class and child rearing in a changing Indian town. *American Ethnologist* 3:783–96.

———. 1983. Household structure and status and expressions of affect in India. *Ethos* 11:263–77.

Singer, Milton. 1959. The great tradition in a metropolitan center: Madras. In M. Singer, ed., *Traditional India: Structure and change,* pp. 141–82. Publications of the American Folklore Society Bibliographical Series, vol. 10.

Thurstone, L. L. 1947. *Multiple factor analysis.* Chicago: University of Chicago Press.

Turner, Victor. 1969. *The ritual process.* Chicago: Aldine Publishing.

Ullrich, Helen E. 1977. Caste differences between Brahmin and non-Brahmin women in a south Indian village. In Alice Schlegel, ed., *Sexual stratification: A cross-cultural view.* New York: Columbia University Press.

Whiting, Beatrice B., ed. 1963. *Six cultures: Studies of child rearing.* New York: John Wiley.

Whiting, B. B., and J. W. M. Whiting. 1975. *Children of six cultures.* Cambridge, Mass.: Harvard University Press.

Whiting, John W. M. 1966. *Field guide for a study of socialization.* New York: John Wiley.

Zucker, R., and F. H. Barron. 1971. Toward a systematic family mythology: The relationship of parents' and adolescents' reports of parent behavior during childhood. Paper presented at the meeting of the Eastern Psychological Association, New York.

Index